When the
WINGS
FALL

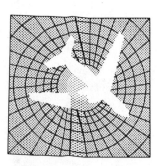

Keith D. Godbey

All scripture quotations are taken from *The Living Bible* (TLB) unless otherwise noted.

First Edition July 1993

When The Wings Fall Off

© 1993 Keith D. Godbey

All rights reserved. No part of this book may be reproduced in any manner without written permission from the author.

Printed in the United States of America

Library of Congress Catalog Card Number: 93-91608

Table of

Contents

Acknowledgments

I am indebted to so many who have given of their time, talent, insight, and tolerance.

I could not have started on this adventure without the counsel, wisdom, and encouragement of my father, Kenneth Godbey, veteran missionary.

A special thanks must go to Judie Showalter, friend and teacher, Rufus Petre, youth leader, Dub Crawford, friend, Ralph Cimino, my second father, and my niece, Natasha Raysik. All contributed of their time, talent, and energies to insure accuracy, providing encouragement at critical junctures.

But most of all, to my wife, Mary Ellen. Her thoughtful insights and feedback, patience with the late night hours of writing, her wonderful sense of humor and unique perspectives, all kept me fresh and energized.

Dedication

(Rev. Kenneth L. Godbey, father of the author, dedicated over fifty years to the ministry. Thirty-nine years were spent in West Africa sharing the message he loved most with those who never heard the name of Jesus. Ken went home to be with the Lord, December 31, 1992.)

You've gone! Yet because of you, I survived.

Your patience, understanding, guidance, and especially your love and prayers, sustained me through the long night. Nothing touched your heart of compassion more quickly than someone who was hurting.

You were so much a part of this writing. In fact, you believed in my "discoveries" more than I, urging their timely completion. Now I understand your urgency.

So Dad, this is for you. Good night! Sleep in His arms. I'll see you in the morning.

About the Author

The son of missionary parents, Captain Godbey spent his formative years growing up on the continent of Africa.

Upon graduation from High School, he returned to the United States to enter college, earning a Bachelor of Science degree. He entered the Air Force and was first stationed with a Strategic Air Command Bomb Wing in Florida. Subsequent assignments allowed participation in the early planning and development stages of a missile wing in California. After successful completion of Air Force duty, he began his career with a major airline as a pilot, the occupation he continues today.

As an author, the thousands of hours of flight experience in commercial jetliners, combined with the Christian heritage of his early years, and matured through personal experience, provide a unique and rich backdrop for this book.

From the Author

Y ou are about to read a personal odyssey. The pain reflected in these pages was real. So are the answers.

If your TV was broken, the best and most logical place to have it repaired would be at its source—the manufacturer. Does it not also make sense, when we are "broken," we too should return to the "manufacturer"? The One who created us, also knows best how to "fix" us emotionally, physically, and spiritually.

When we presume to demand answers from God, we act carelessly. Instead, strive first to know the One who gives the answer. It is then your answers will come. His *still small voice*[1] is most effective when we *listen* to His Word. Often, *God speaks in the language [we] know best—not through [our] ears, but through [our] circumstances.* [2]

Provided at the end of each chapter, are scripture references. I strongly encourage you to use the "Manufacturers Reference Manual," your Bible. Look up each one. Let Him speak directly to you. Experience the thrill of your own new "discoveries." His Word is the REAL source, where you will find REAL answers.

My Word...will achieve the purpose for which I sent it. [3]

He sent forth HIS WORD and HEALED THEM. [4]

References

1   I Kings 19:12 KJV

2   <u>My Utmost for His Highest</u>, Updated Edition, Garborg's Heart 'n Home, January 29. Used by permission.

      Note from the author. Circumstance, like an untrained conscience, can mislead. God may use circumstance to get our attention, but His Word must agree and be the final authority.

3   Isaiah 55:11 NIV

4   Psalms 107:20 NIV

Chapter 1

It Won't EVER
Happen To Me!

They were up next! When they received clearance from the tower, the giant aircraft would slip gracefully onto the runway in preparation for its takeoff roll.

Until this moment, everything had gone smoothly. The passengers settled back in their seats, thankful to be away from the hectic bustle of the airport terminal in the quiet comfort of a modern jetliner. Flight attendants prepared the cabin for flight, checking for seatbacks in the upright position with seatbelts buckled and all baggage safely stowed. In the cockpit checklists were run and it seemed that everything was ready to go. Tonight, however, one small oversight was going to plunge hundreds of friends and relatives into a chilling night of disbelief and despair.

When cleared, the silver bird rolled onto the runway. With the reassuring thunder of the engines, she began to roll toward that moment when she would gracefully begin the climb skyward. But the moments passed and, too late, it became apparent something was terribly wrong. She struggled only a few feet into the air and then came crashing back to earth, breaking apart and strewing twisted pieces of wreckage in her wake. No one survived.

So common to those closely affected by tragedy, the first thought crossing the mind is, "It just can't happen to me—to my family—I must be dreaming! Oh God, please let me wake up!" Then as reality begins to sink in, emotional pain as excruciating as any physical hurt could ever be, begins to pummel and tear, threatening to overwhelm and destroy. You feel the ...*cup of deepest sorrows... rolling [you] in ashes and dirt.. all peace.. all hope is gone and [your] strength has turned to water.* [1]

Across the arid plains of your soul, like a stalking monster, the realization comes that you are alone. No matter how close, caring, or loving, no one can take away your hurt. You must bear it alone and this loneliness only adds to the helpless feeling of impotence and loss of control.

For whatever reason, you are hurting. Coping with today, or even the next few hours and minutes, is anguish seemingly beyond your ability to bear. At this moment you are struggling to survive a tidal wave of sorrow that has crashed into your life, possibly because someone dear has been taken from you by death. You are trying to manage wildly swinging emotions, ranging from despair to acceptance. They threaten to run out of control because your spouse who promised "till death do us part," has suddenly rejected you in favor of greener pastures. Or you may be the victim of abuse, not by strangers, but someone close. Now the rage and betrayal which play across the gamut of your emotions are threatening your mental and physical existence. Perhaps smothering clouds of depression are pressing down with such force that the simple act of standing becomes a struggle. You do not understand or know its source.

Your heart is breaking. *How long must [you hide] daily anguish in your heart* [2] as you try to pretend for friends and acquaintances that everything is O.K.? Your *health is broken and [your] heart is sick...your food tasteless, your appetite gone,* your *tears running down into [your] drink* [3] and your eyes are *red from weeping...because of sadness.* [4]

Facing another long day becomes an overwhelming load. Friends don't understand, and in their efforts to help, they only accentuate the brokenness and pain of your heart. Even when surrounded by people, their chatter, smiles, and laughter, drive deeper the arrow of loneliness which has pierced your soul. And the nights—the nights are worst of all. The dark hours seem to stretch on endlessly. Time crawls slowly by as though enjoying your anguish and despair. Your pillow is soaked with tears and your eyes swollen and red until you wonder if you have any more tears to shed. The walls and ceilings have become a prison cell confining your seemingly futile attempts at prayer. "Why God, where are you—oh God—please H E L P me!" In desperation you try reading His Word, only to find it dry and dusty—dead to your spirit. Your vulnerability may even lead to asking "Does God care?" You become angry as you perceive that He may be ignoring your pleas for help. Feeling betrayed, you are tempted to wonder if God exists.

If you see your dilemma reflected in some small way, then read on! These feelings, and many more, bent the bow of my emotions to the breaking point. Yet with the same absolute certainty of the sunrise, I know He cares. He is with you even when you don't sense His presence. There is healing for your shattered emotions and hope for your future.

If a loving father here on earth gives good things to his child, *won't your Father in heaven even more certainly give good...*[5] to His children? He has promised He *will never, NEVER fail you nor forsake you.* [6] *He is always thinking about you and watching everything that concerns you.* [7] His care goes far beyond our wildest hopes and dreams. In the midst of his agony, the Psalmist understood. *You have seen me tossing and turning through the night. You have collected all my tears and preserved them in your bottle! You have recorded every one in your book.* [8] *When they walk through the Valley of Weeping it will become a place of springs where pools of blessing and refreshment collect after the rains!* [9]

Throughout my life, especially in my professional training as a pilot, I prepared myself to be a self-sufficient person. I took charge and got things done. If you wanted answers, I would get them; expertise, I provided it; a leader, I took charge. I relied on myself and my abilities. With the odds against me, I made the coveted list of pilots for a major airline. If I saw something I wanted and made up my mind to get it, I did. By the time I was in my early 30's, I had joined the ranks of people who could claim, "I have attained all the goals I set for myself." And therein lay the problem.

During the hard driving required for attainment, I rationalized priorities to justify choices. Those choices sacrificed long term values for short term satisfaction. The goals I had set were fine, but I had omitted a vital few. One day, the intricate basket of my life which I had taken such pain to weave, began to unravel. Suddenly, I didn't have an answer—I wasn't in control. All the qualities in which I had taken such pride were mysteriously inadequate. My craft was going down in spite of all I could do. I couldn't believe it. I was going to crash! There wasn't a thing I could do about it...or was there?

No answers were forthcoming from my normally full reservoir of personal ability. The desperation and loneliness, with the regrets of the past, uncertainty of the present, and fear of the future suddenly began to overwhelm me. I know **WHEN THE ENGINES ARE ON FIRE AND THE PLANE IS THREATENING TO FALL OUT OF THE SKY**, there is no room for small talk and games. It's time to get real, to apply correct procedures born out of years of experience and tested by time. The only hope is they will be enough to save the aircraft and ultimately, oneself. Out of the dark and terrifying days, weeks, and months spent searching for answers, I found vital assistance.

The real tragedy is this. Many who face crisis do not realize there is hope and a way out. Procedures and checklists are provided by our Heavenly Father. They have been proven across the centuries by others who have walked those difficult paths before us. They can resolve crisis and guide us through the maze of confusion to the answers we desperately seek. But just as on the flight deck, unless those procedures are applied properly to the crisis, there will be no resolution of the problem.

I do not pretend to be an example of strength and ability. Instead I stand as mute and indisputable evidence to the mercy and grace of my Heavenly Father. It has been His ability to take my life and, in spite of the chaos, bring order into confusion, healing to damaged emotions, and purposeful direction for the future. I know He does care. He has never left my side even during the darkest hours. Best of all, He has a Master Plan He is working out in my life. If He can do this for me, He can do it for you.

Somewhere in the secret corners of your mind, you too have always felt "It just won't happen to me!" But now you find yourself in a struggle for survival. If you are desperately looking for help, struggling to find a way out and needing dependable answers, this book is especially for you.

I know beyond any doubt that He can be trusted with your hurts, your hopes, your past, present, and, most important, your future! Even if the unexpected happens, you can find peace.

For I know the plans I have for you, says the Lord. They are plans for good and not for evil, to give you a future and a hope. In those days when you pray, I will listen. You will find me when you seek me, if you look for me in earnest. [10]

But where does all this lead?

References

1   Lamentations 3:15-19

2   Psalms 13:2

3   Psalms 102:4,10

4   Psalms 31:9-10

5   Matthew 7:11

6   Hebrews 13:5

7   I Peter 5:7

8   Psalms 56:8

9   Psalms 84:6-7

10 Jeremiah 29:11

It Won't EVER
Happen To Me!

Chapter 2

Where In The World Am I Going?

I had never HEARD fear before. Tonight it was there, so real I could almost touch it as it crackled across the airwaves and through the radio.

My flight had left the Dallas/Fort Worth airport earlier that night—destination New York. At 37,000 feet our Boeing 727 was well above the milky overcast. The stars twinkled brightly and the full moon bathed the scene in its soft, flattering light. Visibility was unlimited. Glowing patches created by city lights under the overcast gently reminded us we still belonged to the human race. The only interruption to the soft hum of the instruments was the whistle of the wind slipping swiftly past the windscreen. We felt special. We were being treated to a masterpiece of nature which relatively few people get a chance to observe. Our passengers were snuggled into their respective seats, reading, listening to music, or just sleeping. Even Mother Nature was cooperating. The air was smooth as silk.

"Braniff 235, you listening?" The air traffic controller's voice jolted us back to reality.

"Roger."

"Could you do us a favor? We think we may have lost one. Could you check and see if you pick up an ELT?" [1]

"You bet. Hold on a minute." We quickly turned the frequency to monitor the Emergency Channel. Nothing—just silence.

In the next few moments, we pieced the story together. The pilot of a small, single-engine plane, with his wife and children on board, had become disoriented. Too late he had learned his destination was covered by overcast. Not being instrument rated, he was unable to descend through the cloud layer. He did not have enough fuel to return to his point of departure. After calling Center and searching for alternatives, suddenly the airways had gone silent. All efforts by Center to re-establish communication were proving futile.

"Braniff, can you try one more thing for me? See if you can raise him."

With that, the controller gave us the last frequency the aircraft had been on and his call sign. We switched frequencies quickly and, as I put the mike to my mouth, glanced at the other crew members. Each was staring at me, knowing we would probably get no answer.

"Cessna 456 - this is Braniff 235. Can you hear me?" All that followed was a deafening silence.

"Cessna 456 - this is Braniff 235. Center is trying to reach you. Can I help in any way?"

The speaker suddenly came alive with two words. In them was the sum total of fear, prayer, and hope.

"Oh...GOD............!" Then silence.

There was no doubt. That flight and family were in desperate trouble. Quickly I called again, exercising all possible control in my own voice to reassure, my goal to get the pilot calm and thinking. After a couple of quick radio exchanges, we determined that he was still flying, totally lost, and on the verge. The "verge of what" was our concern. Slowly, he calmed to the point at which we were at least communicating. With each transmission we could hear the cries of his family in the background, his voice reflecting clearly the desperation and fear he was fighting.

As we circled overhead, the story slowly emerged. While talking with Center, he had seen what he thought was an opening in the cloud layer and endeavored to descend through it. But as visual reference to the horizon disappeared, he had lost control. The aircraft entered a "death spiral." [2] Miraculously the aircraft broke out below the clouds. He had somehow managed to regain control before hitting the ground or ripping the wings off. He was now in a valley, covered by the overcast, totally surrounded by mountains with no apparent passage through which he could escape to a safe landing. In his mind, having escaped death once, he and his family were still doomed.

As quickly as possible without further confusion, we had him tune in different radio facilities. He managed to give us the direction and distance to each. These were quickly passed on to Center, who plotted his location. The words of the controller after identifying the aircraft position were simply, "That man owes a big 'thank you' to Someone." If the spiral had taken place just a few miles in any direction, that family would have been picked up in baskets off the peaks of the Blue Ridge Mountains.

During our exchange with the small aircraft, we had maintained contact with Center. They were now asking if we could possibly descend, accept a vector to the distressed aircraft's location, and lead it out of the valley. However, after determining the maximum speed of the small plane, we knew there was just no way. Even by slowing to landing speed, with our flaps extended to allow the slowest possible flight speed, our big jet would simply not stay airborne and allow that small craft to keep pace with us. Another prop-driven airliner had been monitoring our conversations and felt their plane could do it. The crew quickly volunteered and headed in the direction of the lost plane. Center thanked us for our help, and released us to continue our flight to New York. It was one night our passengers didn't mind being late. They had been a part of something important.

It was not until the next day we learned the outcome of that near tragedy. The other airliner, with the help of Center, had found the small plane circling and led him through the pass to a nearby airport. The small plane with its precious family cargo had landed safely.

The initial reaction is to wonder why a pilot would allow himself to get into such a compromising position? Didn't he check the weather before he left? Couldn't he see the overcast as he proceeded with his flight?

I am certain the man was a reasonably good pilot. After all, to obtain a license, he had passed some very rigid requirements. I am sure he was a responsible family man and provided for them well. Most of all, he had displayed courage of character. He had proven it by overcoming fear and panic when it counted most. So if all this is true, how did he get into his situation?

We can only speculate.

Our pilot friend probably made a superficial check of the weather. He may have asked if the destination weather was good for flying but failed to see there was still overcast through which he would be required to pass. If he didn't know about the overcast, he naturally would not have been alarmed about crossing mountains and then getting back down. Once airborne and during the flight, everything went smoothly. He may have been enjoying the same "magic of the moon" which we had, just going with the easy flow, staying above the clouds. He was probably enjoying the company of his family, chatting with his wife, teasing the children.

But then came the time for descent and landing. The rules say that you must stay in the clear, away from clouds both vertically and horizontally. In other words, you fly visually. An instrument pilot is required to have many additional hours of training. He must be able to control an airplane and follow very specific routes simply by looking at a cluster of needles and gauges. It's embarrassing if you pop out of the clouds upside down. But our pilot friend had not prepared himself for instrument flight, so when he lost his reference to the horizon, he was no longer able to maintain control of his aircraft. He had neither deliberately planned to put his family in jeopardy nor willfully tried to break the rules. He had just "gone with the flow" as so many do. Without realizing it, he had stepped beyond his capabilities, beyond the scope of his preparation, into the middle of crisis. Miraculously, he and his family survived.

Too often, life imitates. Through high school and college, as long as things are going well, the course of least resistance is followed. Easy decisions are made. After all, we are taught from early childhood, "Don't rock the boat!" We follow the crowd, learning to play to our critics, our peers who either accept or reject us. Rejection forces us to deal with many additional problems. Acceptance is so much easier.

Human beings do not like the constraints of discipline. When told to reconsider our actions in light of the future or eternity, we resent it. Eternity! That's even worse. To think of eternity, we have to consider our mortality—death! Ugh! Such an ugly subject. Later! Later! We don't have time for that now. And so, without realizing it, with no malicious intent, our priorities are diverted; our goals diluted.

We look instead for the fun and laughter. Everything is going great. Early goals I have set are realized. I begin to see myself in the light of my own standards—standards which my crowd has set because that is where we are. If my friends approve, I am happy and accepted. I progress socially and professionally. My self image begins to shine and I see myself as someone special, a person that has it together. Of course, my friends let me know just how "together" I am. My education, my children's achievements, the house I have purchased in the right neighborhood, the way I provide for my family, all let me know I'm really O.K.

We may encounter a ripple—a business deal goes sour, a friend gets sick. We hesitate in our headlong pursuit of happiness and success, realizing momentarily that after all, we are mortal.

So we pause, considering our destination. We may even start going to church. After all, it is the social thing to do. We really are good, community oriented folks—religious. If the ripple gets closer to home, maybe even splashes into our little boat, we spend a couple of minutes in prayer, trying to cut a deal with God. We let Him know how good we are and how much good we can do for Him. We may even make promises to clean up our act if God will just help us out. Things smooth out, everything is sunny and rosy again, and we forget our commitments. Paul understood this tendency when he said, *If you are thinking, 'Oh, I would never behave like that'—let this be a warning to you. For you too may fall...*[3]

The activities we pursue in our preparation for life are good. But there comes a point at which we must lay out a plan. That plan should target our ultimate destination with priorities in correct order to best help us attain those goals. Deviation from that set of priorities leads to failure.

It would have been ridiculous for me, the very first time I took a flying lesson, to insist on flying a jet. If all I ever trained in was a glider, it would be equally ridiculous for me to insist on being the Captain.

As a pilot, I must periodically go to the company training center. There, for three long arduous days, I am subjected to rigorous testing. Each time in the simulator, we are given emergencies: engine failures, engine fires, hydraulic leaks, depressurization, gear collapsing on landing, deteriorating weather, and many, many more. With each passing year, even though I know basically what is coming, a new wrinkle or set of circumstances teaches me something new. The depth of my preparation increases. Now if a real emergency is encountered, I am fully prepared and less likely to fail when lives depend upon my skill.

But now assume that at each simulator period, my instructor only gives me hydraulic problems. Year after year, I get better and better until my training is perfect when it comes to hydraulic problems. Then one day, with 200 passengers sitting behind me, relying on my preparation and expertise to take them safely to their destination, I have an engine failure. I am an excellent pilot; I am prepared—but only for hydraulic problems.

You see, I meant no harm. I worked hard to be good; my preparation was excellent. But it was also limited. My priorities had been out of kilter, and now I am beyond the scope of my preparation.

So it is with our lives. All our good-intentioned achievements don't count, if, in the final analysis, our priorities in preparation leave out some vital part. When we build the structure of our lives, there must first be a foundation, and that foundation must be capable of holding the structure to be placed upon it.

King Solomon, one of the wisest men of history, knew that without a solid foundation, the structure could not withstand the winds of stress. So he instructed, *in everything you do, put God first, and he will direct you and crown your efforts with success.* [4] Jesus added emphasis to this. He was trying to help us build a solid foundation upon which to place the structure of our lives. He addressed concerns and worries, the same ones we still carry about today. Where will I live? What clothes do I need? Where is the next meal coming from? We get so caught up in the need to secure answers that we deviate from our plan. *Your heavenly Father already knows perfectly well that you need them, and he will give them to you if you give him FIRST place in your life and live as he wants you to. So don't be anxious about tomorrow. God will take care of your tomorrow too. Live one day at a time.* [5] How beautifully simple and effective!

The day will come in your life, through no fault of your own, when you will be confronted with a set of circumstances beyond your capabilities, just like the pilot, suddenly confronted with a situation for which he is untrained. The foundation of his preparation could not pass the testing demanded of his skill.

It is essential to establish a foundation upon which we can build the structure of our lives. When circumstance begins to tear at the fabric we have woven, we can rest assured the foundation will stand, because the preparation was correct. If we place our relationship with our Heavenly Father as top priority, our remaining goals will take their good and proper place, preparing us for the full and abundant life we desire.

You fall on hard times, suffer setbacks, or experience emotional pain from some crisis in your life. People try to suggest there must be something wrong with you. Maybe you need to confess some hidden sin in your life so God can continue to bless you.

If you are suffering hurt, already depressed spiritually, emotionally, or physically, thinking that God has somehow selected you to be the recipient of His displeasure is cruel and unnecessary. It is not my place nor that of others to judge,[6] for that prerogative belongs to God alone; nor is it my duty to convince of some sin [7], for that is the responsibility of the Holy Spirit. My instructions are precise and clear; I am to help you carry your burden, with compassion and love. [8]

Hundreds of years ago, the Psalmist wrote, *the good man does not escape all troubles—he has them too. But the Lord helps him in each and every one.* [9] King David was called a *man after God's own heart*; [10] yet if you read Psalms 42, David was in the middle of deep depression. Peter agreed when he wrote, *don't be bewildered or surprised when you go through the fiery trials ahead, for this is no strange,*

226009

unusual thing that is going to happen to you. [11] Look also at the parable by Jesus in Luke 6:47-49. The floods (trials) came on both the good and the bad alike. The only difference is that one foundation remained intact while the other crumbled. Jesus understood "life is no bed of roses." *I have told you all this so that you will have peace of heart and mind. Here on earth you will have many trials and sorrows; but cheer up, for I have overcome the world.* [12]

So how do we start this plan of preparation?

First, start with your priorities—make God the most important priority in your life. You may already have made a commitment to Christ, but your priorities have become diluted. Stop and re-examine them now. Make certain this vital, first building block is properly in place.

Possibly you have never examined or been presented with the claims of Christ on each life. You may face the same dilemma which confronted Martin Luther when he nailed his Manifesto to the church door hundreds of years ago. If you do not know Jesus Christ as Lord and Savior, I encourage you to read "Luther's Dilemma" (Chapter 9) before you proceed further.

Second, problems should not surprise you. Trials are a fact of life. But when priorities are correct, God will turn the negative of your pain into a glowing example of His grace working in your life. Even though you may feel things are out of control, God is still very much in control.

Perhaps *floods of sorrow pour upon [you] like a thundering cataract,* [13] and the torrents are threatening to sweep your fragile craft away in their rushing cascades. You are barely hanging on emotionally, wondering if you will make it, and if anyone cares. The answer is YES! YES, you can make it! YES, someone cares!

You have seen me tossing and turning through the night. You have COLLECTED ALL MY TEARS and preserved them in your bottle! You have RECORDED EVERY ONE in your book.[14]

With priorities set and a firm foundation built, you're now ready to press forward. Come on! Let's go file our flight plan.

References

1   Emergency Locator Transmitter - Sends out a distinctive signal
     when activated to assist search aircraft in locating downed
     aircraft

2   The aircraft enters a tight descending turn, picking up speed
     and stress on the airframe. It will either eventually hit the
     ground or pull a wing off from the "G" forces.

3   I Corinthians 10:12

4   Proverbs 3:6

5   Matthew 6:32-34

6   Matthew 7:1, Romans 2:5

7   Galatians 5:16, Romans 8:26

8   Galatians 6:1-2, James 5:16

9   Psalms 34:19

10   Acts 13:22

11   I Peter 4:12

12   John 16:33

13   Psalms 42:7

14   Psalms 56:8

Chapter 3

Better File
The Flight Plan

I remember so well the first flight plan I ever filed. My instructor, an old, grizzly ex-Navy pilot, had informed me that I was going to take him cross-country the next day. He had pointed out the spot on the map, a ranch with a small grass strip out in the middle of nowhere, about fifty miles from the airport of departure. I was thrilled; I knew I was ready.

At home that evening, I pored over the maps, checked weather forecasts, obtained the frequencies I would need, plotted headings, distances, and expected time enroute. I had taken everything into account. At least I thought I had.

The next morning, bright and early, I reported to the airport. My instructor, still nursing a cup of coffee, mumbled something about being ready. I assured him I was. He pointed at the airplane we were to use, and I proceeded with my preflight inspection of the aircraft. Just as I was finishing, he came ambling over, climbed into the right seat, grunted something about my taking too long, and then rotated his finger. That meant, "Let's get this show on the road."

I taxied out, did my engine checks, then pulled out onto the runway for takeoff. The takeoff roll was perfect as we lifted off into the "wild blue" in superb fashion. I was feeling somewhat smug to have done such a brilliant job. My instructor, certain we were a safe distance above the ground and assured I wasn't going to kill him, promptly leaned back and went to sleep. Undaunted, I took up my heading and checked the time. I'd show him just how a good pilot did things.

At precisely the right time, I began checking to find the ranch. It wasn't there! Oh well, it must be just a little further. However, just to make sure, I started a slow "S" turn so I could observe the ground on both sides of the airplane. There was nothing that looked even vaguely familiar. My heart was starting to pump a little faster and for some funny reason, the wheel was getting sticky. After another five minutes, I turned back. I must have missed my time check and flown past the ranch. But it was still nowhere to be found. About this time, the "thing" woke up.

"We there yet?"

"Well, the time's up, but I can't seem to locate it." I desperately wanted to find it without his help.

"Well, well. Someone must have moved it." With this sarcastic observation, he closed his eyes and went back to sleep. After I floundered around for another fifteen minutes becoming more and more disoriented, he finally came back to life.

"Well, you gonna' find it or sit up here until you run out of gas?"

Embarrassed, I finally admitted I might need just a little help.

"Son, if you can't find out where you got me, and get me where I wanna' go, then you got no biznes flyn' planes. Now why don't you look out the window, then look at that there map, and decide where it is you got me. Then make up your mind where you wanna' take me. Unnerstan'?"

My face flushed with humiliation, but I did what he said. In my earlier confusion with concentration focused on "seeing" the ranch, I had ignored two very prominent landmarks which showed me immediately where I was on the map. When I realized my location, I felt so small I could have stood up straight and walked under an ant without bumping my head. On a fifty mile cross-country leg, I had missed my target by fifteen miles; now that's not easy to do! Once oriented, I turned and in a few minutes, we arrived at the ranch.

"O.K., let's go home!" And with that, he went back to sleep.

It was not until much later that I found out why I had had so much trouble. It was his habit, with first time cross-country students, to go out to the plane and bend a tab on the rudder. This caused the aircraft to constantly "pull" to the right. Since it had no trim tab which would have enabled me to correct this tendency, plus my being an inexperienced student, I allowed the aircraft to slowly but surely wander off course. One thing was certain, if I had not been able to recover, I would never have touched one of his airplanes again. Also, he had never gone to sleep—he was enjoying my discomfort too much. But what a valuable lesson he had taught.

The only reason I was able to salvage the situation, was that I had filed a flight plan. It had forced me to think, to investigate, and to plan for any eventuality, to know the terrain. I had studied the map, but in my confusion during flight, had overlooked some important clues because I had not gone back to basics. My instructor was not about to bail me out. He could not have cared less about my cross-country skill.

He wanted to see how I would react to the stress of being lost when I was alone. First I had to face the reality I was lost and admit I needed help. His advice to "look out the window" was his way of making me break through the confusion and start thinking. If he had told me which way to go, I would have not learned the valuable lesson he wanted me to grasp. When mistakes are made, I can correct them if I will get the basic priorities back into proper order.

We often expect God to "bail us out," yet we seldom take the time to file our flight plan in order to determine what His purpose is for our lives. God revealed to Adam and Eve His perfect plan for happiness and fulfillment. They felt they knew a better way and took it, thus alienating themselves from their Source of Life.

People born today have this same choice. We can either accept His way, realizing His perfect plan for our lives, or we can choose to pursue our own goals. This will result in a dilution of our priorities and confusion in reaching our destination. Jeremiah knew that man was not capable of mapping his own course. *I know it is not within the power of man to map his life and plan his course—so you correct me, Lord; but please be gentle.* [1] God's assurance today, as it was to Jeremiah, is ... *I know the plans I have for you...* [2] Not even God will leave something as important as our lives to chance; there is a meticulous plan outlining every detail.

Everyone in the aviation industry knows the person responsible for the flight plan is the pilot-in-command, the captain. Since God already has a plan for your life, if you proceed to file your own, in effect you are telling God that He is not in command of your life. That is where problems begin.

So what is this plan? His rules and laws have been written in every human heart. [3] These rules were given to Moses in the form of the Ten Commandments. [4] If you examine their content, you will find that the first four deal with our relationship to God, the last six with our relationship and attitudes toward ourselves and others.

The very first commandment demands that you put God first. King Solomon [5] and Jesus [6] both re-emphasized this first and most important step. We must first be

RECONCILED TO OUR HEAVENLY FATHER!

Problems and testing are not a sign of hidden sin. However, honesty is essential in your evaluation of your relationship with God. Early in my crisis, God gave me a scripture which proved to be my life preserver. I clung to it tenaciously, reminding God almost hourly of His promise. Yet, as the emotional pain increased and sleep eluded me, it seemed that God ignored me. I was receiving no answers. My prayers seemed to fall back in my face. I went back to the promise, reading and rereading, *when you pray, I will listen. You will find me when you seek me.* [7] Slowly through the fog of desperation I realized that there was more to the verse. It ended with the words,

IF you look for me in earnest.

I was indignant. God, how could I not be in earnest when I am hurting like this? His answer soon became clear. "I don't want your sacrifice—I want YOU!" At first I didn't understand. I had been trying to put my life in order for months. I had made commitments and was doing my best to put them into action. Slowly, I realized that my commitments, even though honest, had been superficial. I was still trying to make deals with God, trying to tell Him how I thought my life should be run. My "sacrifices" of commitment were not enough. He wanted to be Lord of my life, and I was having a hard time stepping down from being the captain. God wasn't going to settle for copilot.

Mine was not a sin of commission but one of omission. I was being conditional, unwilling to give Him total control. To cope with life or the crisis in which I found myself, this first step in preparing my flight plan was absolutely essential. I had to be willing to allow Him total and complete control of my life. There can only be one captain. He accepted nothing less from His own Son. *Even though Jesus was God's Son, He had to learn from experience what it was like to obey, [even] when obeying meant suffering.* [8]

The moment I willingly gave unconditional control to the Holy Spirit, I began to receive the help I so desperately needed. Immediately, His Word came alive. Now, because He was able to communicate, my healing process began. I was able to respond to His prompting.

You chart the path ahead of me, and tell me where to stop and rest. Every moment you know where I am...You saw me before I was born and scheduled each day of my life...every day was recorded in your Book. How precious it is, Lord, to realize that you are thinking about me constantly. [9]

The moment you accept this powerful concept, simply ask Him to take control. He has promised, *if we confess our sins to Him, He can be depended on to forgive us and to cleanse us from every wrong.* [10]

Few who try to put our lives in order have a problem with this step. We quickly recognize and accept God's love and forgiveness. Now comes the second and equally important step in the preparation of the flight plan, that of being

RECONCILED TO YOURSELF!

When initiating this step, many of us run into problems. Several years ago it was necessary for me to have surgery. During the last visit to my doctor prior to surgery, I asked if the work he was about to do would be classified as "major" or "minor" surgery. With a wry grin he stated, "Well, if it's on me, it's major. On you, it's minor!"

That is exactly how many of us react to God. We believe God can and will forgive us and He can and will provide answers to prayer for others. However, when applying these same principles to ourselves, it becomes "major" surgery and our faith falters. We experience His forgiveness and feel the joy of sins forgiven. Yet, in spite of His grace, we continue to hold grudges against ourselves.

Why? Is it because we know ourselves too well? Dad would often state, "There are only two that you can't fool—God and yourself."

We were there when the mistakes resulting in hurts, alienation, and rejection were made. Memory pulls us back into the agony of recrimination, thinking, "If only...!" Realizing we contributed to some of our own problems, we now see ourselves as flawed and imperfect. Self-confidence diminishes as self-esteem sinks lower and lower. We begin to wonder why God has bothered with those as insignificant and imperfect as we.

Slowly but surely, the mind is sucked deeper into this whirlpool of destructive thinking which soon begins to reflect in our actions and physical demeanor. The face reflects the hurt of damaged emotions and the fatigue of sleepless nights. Shoulders sag with the burden of problems and footsteps no longer reflect the spring of purpose as we drag ourselves to accomplish only the vital necessities of life. With a look in the mirror, we become even more critical of our physical selves, appearance, circumstance, and station in life. Next comes the horrible trap of comparative thinking—comparing what we have or don't have to what others around us seem to be enjoying. If we have suffered the loss of someone close, the sight of another couple sharing and laughing together can plunge the heart and mind into a cesspool of self-pity. The next step is inevitable. *I stoop with sorrow and with shame. I am scorned by all my enemies and even more by my neighbors and friends. They dread meeting me and look the other way when I go by. I am forgotten like a dead man, like a broken and discarded pot.*[11]

Of course, we fail to see our friends' new attitude in its true light; we are incapable of understanding. Even though they are concerned and want to help, they are afraid of the unknown. The possibility of hurting you further causes them to retreat. We perceive their actions as further rejection, opening the wounds of loneliness until they are bleeding and raw. Self-esteem continues its plunge through the basement of our soul. This self-perpetuating "death spiral" of emotions will continue until we realize that because we are reconciled to our Heavenly Father, we can now be reconciled to ourself!

Close friends riding in a car with me are constantly amazed at how lost I become in a city. If I am able to fly coast to coast and touch down at a specific airport with pinpoint accuracy, how in the world do I get so lost in a "little" city? For some reason my sense of direction is nil on the ground. I explain that up high, my perspective is much different. I don't see just a street, I see the whole city. Moreover, I have precise instruments which take me by the hand to my exact destination. My perspective is different!

To become reconciled to ourselves, we must readjust our perspectives and understand how God sees us and how much He values us.

Even though He knew we would ultimately reject Him, He still ...*loved [us] so much, that He gave His only Son.*[12] He gave His greatest Treasure, His Son, as a sacrifice so we could be reconciled to Him.

Because of that sacrifice, God places a high premium on what His Son did for us. Now there is *no condemnation* [13] hanging over our heads. In fact, you are *brought into the very presence of God, and you are standing there before Him with nothing left against you, nothing left that He could even chide you for!*[14] Without any doubt, *we are his children...for all God gives to His Son Jesus is now ours too.* [15]

Stop to think of the implications. Because of Christ's atonement, not only are the sins and faults forgiven and cast into the sea of forgetfulness, but we have been made members of the Royal Family with equal privilege. Now we *can come fearlessly right into God's presence, assured of His glad welcome.* [16] This is our heritage!

At first, I had difficulty with this concept. There were actions which I could have taken long ago which might have altered the course of events. Memories still haunted me and painful emotions still tried to conquer me. But as I began to see that He had forgiven me, not because of anything I had done but because of Christ's merit and goodness, I realized that I must turn those memories and emotions over to Him. My unwillingness to allow His healing, showed my priority of self concern; I was being selfish.

The only other issue was trust. If I had to forget the past, it meant I would have to face and deal with today. Was I afraid of stepping forward with my life, afraid I would fail again?

In either case I was wrong. Selfishness would only prolong my hurt and hinder His loving involvement in my life. Fear of failure and lack of trust in my Heavenly Father's ability prevented giving Him full control. He had already promised I could *do everything God asks me to with the help of Christ.*[17]

But there was an even more important reason. No matter how isolated we may try to be, we are still *known and read by everybody.*[18] Could my self-centered attitude and fear prevent others from seeing His hand at work in my life? Am I acting as if I know more than God, justifying holding grudges against myself?

Lastly, if my Father thinks I am worthy of forgiveness, happiness, and hope for the future, how dare I not forgive myself? How dare I not act like the person He wants me to be? *So take a new grip with your tired hands, and stand firm on your shaky legs, and mark out a straight, smooth path for your feet so that those who follow You, though weak and lame, will not fall and hurt themselves, but become strong.*[19]

"But God, how can I possibly help anyone else when I feel worthless, when I'm hurting, depressed, or lonely?" His answer, *I am with you; that is all you need. My power shows up best in weak people.*[20] *Your strength must come from the Lord's mighty power within you.*[21]

God made us winners! Realize this wonderful truth and start acting like a winner. When we think we are down and out, we are most vulnerable, knowing we must trust and depend on Him. This is the exact time when God's possibilities are most likely to happen!

The saying goes, "You really know your friends when the chips are down." Everyone talks about love. Yet, right now you may be hurting because "love" failed you, leaving you lonely and vulnerable. This is not how the Love of God works. *Nothing can ever separate us from his love. Death can't, and life can't. The angels won't, and all the powers of Hell itself cannot keep God's love away. Our fears for today, our worries about tomorrow, or where we are—high above [in] the sky, or in the deepest ocean—nothing—Nothing— NOTHING! will ever be able to separate us from the LOVE of God.*[22]

We are *His prize!* [23] He is so concerned about our welfare, *He protects you day and night. He keeps you from all evil, and preserves your life. He keeps his eye upon you as you come and go, and always guards you!* [24]

I was obsessed with what I perceived to be my life in shambles. How could I ever be happy, feel fulfilled again? During prayer time one day, the Holy Spirit softly answered, *Because he loves me, I will rescue him...when he calls on me, I will answer; I will be with him in trouble...I will satisfy him with a full life.* [25]

If you are feeling down and out, with nothing left in your future—STOP! You are special! You are a winner! You do have a future! Start acting like a child of the King and member of the Royal Family. God has provided forgiveness. Now forgive yourself! You may have made mistakes, but when we see our failures, *the more we see God's abounding grace forgiving us!* [26]

Don't sell yourself short. Remember, you are a winner!

Finally, to complete your flight plan, be

RECONCILED TO OTHERS.

Our enemy is so devious. If he can't get you down on yourself, he will target your mind on someone else. As I began to deal with forgiving myself, it suddenly seemed that I could trace almost every cause of my problem to one person. I wanted to let that person know just what I thought of him, how awful and hurtful I felt he had been.

However, resentment, anger, and nursing vendettas only hurt me. *It is mine to avenge, I will repay.* [27] My anger and unforgiving spirit were hurting only me. *Never criticize or condemn [judge]—or it will come back on you. Go easy on others; then they will do the same for you...whatever measure you use to give—large or small—will be used to measure what is given back to you.* [28]

Worse yet, my unforgiving attitude was inhibiting my communication with my Heavenly Father. *If you are standing before the altar.. and suddenly remember that a friend has something against you, leave your sacrifice there beside the altar and go and apologize and be reconciled to him, and then come and offer your sacrifice to God.* [29] If I do not maintain clear channels of communications with Him, how can I expect my prayers to be answered? Jesus said, *Your strong love for each other will prove to the world that you are my disciples.*[30] That love is for friends and enemies alike.

If we want God's forgiveness, *be gentle and ready to forgive; never hold grudges. Remember, the Lord forgave you, so you must forgive others.* [31] To receive forgiveness we must give forgiveness in equal measure—unconditionally. Don't be a "bead collector." [32] Instead, *be kind to each other, tenderhearted, forgiving one another, just as God has forgiven you because you belong to Christ.* [33]

"But I just can't forgive them for what they did!"

You're right! But God can! With His help you can give that hurt to Him for resolution. Remember, God sees more than you and I see. He looks at the heart. The very person against whom you are holding anger and resentment needs Jesus and His peace just as you do. They are just as important to Him as you and I. Jesus taught us to *love your enemies! Pray for those who persecute you!* [34]

Psychologist Archibald Hart clearly stated, "**Forgiveness is surrendering my right to hurt you for hurting me.**"

Don't let the cancer of grudges rob you of God's best in your life. Let him handle them. I have more than enough to do just keeping my relationship with my Heavenly Father, myself, and others pure and good. Remember, *weeping may go on all night, but in the morning there is joy!* [35]

Happy are those...who want above all else to follow your steps. When they walk through the Valley of Weeping it will become a place of springs where pools of blessing and refreshment collect after rains! [36]

Unfortunately I do not remember the source, but written in the fly leaf of my Bible are the following words -

"Without God, I can't; and Without Me, God won't!"

This is your chance to fly or crash! Which will it be? It's your choice.

References

1   Jeremiah 10:23-24

2   Jeremiah 29:11

3   Romans 2:14

4   Exodus 20

5   Proverbs 3:6

6   Matthew 6:32-34

7   Jeremiah 29:12, 13

8   Hebrews 5:8

9   Psalms 139:3,16,17

10 I John 1:9

11 Psalms 31:10-12

12 John 3:16, Romans 5:8

13 Romans 8:1

14 Colossians 1:22

15 Romans 8:17

16 Ephesians 3:12

17 Philippians 4:13

18 II Corinthians 3:2 NIV

19 Hebrews 12:12-13

20 II Corinthians 12:9

21 Ephesians 6:10

22 Romans 8:38-39

23 Psalms 94:14

24 Psalms 121:6-8

25 Psalms 91:14-16

26 Romans 5:20

27 Hebrews 10:30 NIV

28 Luke 6:37-38

29 Matthew 5:23-24

30 John 13:35

31 Colossians 3:13

32 A phrase used by a psychologist friend to describe someone who collects grudges (beads) and faithfully recounts them each day to make certain they never forget.

33 Ephesians 4:32

34 Matthew 5:44

35 Psalms 30:5

36 Psalms 84:5-6

Chapter 4

In A Crunch OR Going To Crunch?

The sleek jet moved slowly onto the runway. Cleared for takeoff, the mammoth engines started their thunderous growl as the huge craft began its lumbering run to liftoff. At the precise predetermined speed, she lifted into the air, transformed instantly from an awkward gargantuan into a graceful, soaring eagle. With a gentle climbing turn, she turned northward, carrying within her silver hull, the lives of 300.

As passengers settled into the security of their respective cocoons of activity, the sinister finger of fate was already writing its script. Still climbing to cruise altitude within 100 miles of the departure airport, the first alarm sounded.

Far in the back, smoke drifted lightly into the cabin. Flight attendants quickly tried to locate its source, while another notified the flight deck. The engineer left his station to investigate, but upon arriving at the scene, the smoke had all but dissipated. The only abnormality was an excessive warmth of the cabin. Returning to the flight deck, he checked all instruments and warning indicators. Because nothing abnormal was found, no decision for action was made. Precious moments were allowed to slip away. Choices were either delayed or never made.

Suddenly, dark, choking, toxic clouds of smoke broke some invisible barrier and came billowing into the aft cabin, driving passengers forward. Somewhere deep in her belly, the graceful lady was burning, consuming herself and threatening those who rode in her.

Only then was the decision made to return and land. However, it became a desperate race between the lady's self destruction and the safety of the runway and evacuation. Radio contact was made and emergency equipment notified. They took up stations along the runway at a point where the stricken craft should come to rest. With agonizing slowness, as if suspended in an oily dream of slow motion, she made her approach to the two-mile strip of safety. Her touchdown was perfect.

Instead of stopping near them, the captain allowed the big bird to roll slowly past the fire equipment and the horrified fire crews. They took up pursuit like so many desperate ducklings trying to catch their mother. The aircraft continued its roll for almost another mile to the end of the runway. As it turned off and pulled to a stop, the tower was still in contact with the crew.

Precious minutes slipped away and were forever lost as the emergency equipment raced to reach the ill-fated craft. When it finally arrived, the engines were still running, preventing the fire fighters from initiating fire and rescue procedures. But now, the airwaves had become ghostly silent. We can only imagine the horror and terror that filled the cabin as toxic fumes insidiously took their toll. All 300 souls, including crew, perished.

The consequence of choice is seldom more apparent or dramatic than in the world of aviation. To an even greater degree, the air is terribly unforgiving of those who regard it with nonchalance and carelessness. The demanding trio of responsibility, choice, and accountability requires that those who enter the sanctuary of flight maintain constant vigilance to assure safe passage.

No less certain are the consequences of choices which each of us make. From early youth, we are faced with decisions in almost every aspect of our lives. Some of us had the rich heritage of parents, teachers, and pastors who taught us the importance of choice and the necessity of priorities. They guided our steps, helping us to avoid the numerous pitfalls and traps which await the unwary. Others not so fortunate were left to stroll the wide, non-demanding road which leads to spiritual alienation, never realizing that God's Law of Harvest would one day require accountability. The tragic result can be seen all around, evident in the wreckage of human lives strewn along the runways of life. Still others, though given the opportunity and guidance, chose to plot their own courses and learn through bitter experience.

Each time a sleek jet glides down a runway and ultimately lifts gracefully into the air, the effects of the applied laws of physics and aerodynamics are witnessed. Without a thorough understanding and application of these laws, the world of aviation would still be a primitive art.

Of greater importance are the laws of God which have been put into place and applied to each human life. These laws were designed by a loving Heavenly Father. They provide a foundation on which to base decisions and choices, to help us navigate the treacherous channels through which we must pass. *Don't be misled; remember that you can't ignore God and get away with it: a [person] will always reap just the kind of crop [they] sow!* [1] Consequence is a reality of choice.

For many years, the captain's voice was the final and only voice heard in the cockpit. However, after the investigation of countless accidents, investigators found that many times other pilots sat silently by as fateful decisions were made which resulted in tragedy. Fear of usurping "captain's authority" had prevented their timely input to prevent the accident. This abdication of responsibility did not relieve accountability for the ultimate safety of the flight. Now, even though the Captain is leader, the "crew concept" is utilized, placing equal responsibility on each crew member. The crew must mesh together as a team, checking and double-checking the other's actions. Only with this awareness of the flight environment is maximum safety attained.

In hindsight this "crew concept" is so logical. Yet we often see reflected in our own attitudes, the desire to abdicate responsibility. In effect, we allow others to make choices for us, hoping we then have an excuse if something goes wrong. We take the easy way out, going along with the crowd. After all, "Everyone is doing it!" So, instead of examining the consequence of a choice as it relates to our life, we bow to choices made by others. We fail to seize our opportunities to follow Christ and His plan for our life. Those "other" people have no interest or investment in your life; therefore, they have no concern for the consequences of those choices and how they may effect your well-being.

God's plan is different. He *rewards each one of us according to the work we do...* [2] *I tell you this, that you must give account on Judgment Day for every idle word you speak...either you will be justified by them or you will be*

---

condemned. [3] Clearly, God holds us directly responsible and accountable for the choices we make or avoid.

During the investigation of this accident, it became apparent the captain had allowed other crew members to skip or eliminate critical portions of the checklist. He failed to give direction in other areas which could have resulted in lives being saved. However, even this obvious abdication of responsibility did not eliminate the terrible consequences. He lost his own life.

This is a critical crossroad. You must consciously make a decision. Putting it off is in fact a decision against yourself. These decisions are essential in addressing your spiritual, emotional, and physical needs. Vacillation leads only to confusion and frustration, delaying the healing so desperately needed for the emotional hurt and pain in which you are immersed. *A doubtful mind will be as unsettled as a wave of the sea that is driven and tossed by the wind; every decision you then make will be uncertain, as you turn first this way, and then that.* [4] You must accept accountability for your actions or you literally tie the hands of God and prevent His meaningful intervention in your life. Thus you cannot *expect the Lord to give you any solid answers.* [4]

The uncommitted, unstructured, and undisciplined life that just "goes with the flow," is not His plan. He has so much more planned for you. *My purpose is to give life in all its fullness,* [5] a meaningful, abundant, and directed life. He wants to use your life to attract others to Himself through the glowing example of His love and grace reflected in you.

As you view humanity, you will see many living with no direction, no purpose, and no meaning. People are moving at top speed but going nowhere. They work from early morning till late night just to make ends meet, but find little true satisfaction in their accomplishments. They are on a huge merry-go-round, traveling in the same old ruts until one tragic day the "music" stops. They are left holding nothing as their world crashes down around them in choking clouds of dust.

Without His direction, all preparation to build the foundation of life will have left out vital ingredients. The priorities set down by God to put Him first, are ignored. Consequently, subsequent choices and decisions fail to accomplish their desired purpose. We are left feeling scattered, unattached, rootless—adrift in a sea of bewilderment, wondering who we are and where we are going.

Thousands of years ago, Elijah confronted this problem when he challenged the nation of Israel, *How long are you going to waver between two opinions? If the Lord is God, then follow Him!* [6] On another occasion, Joshua faced the same problem. *Decide today whom you will obey.* [7] This undecided or scattered condition has plagued the human race for centuries.

Webster's Dictionary defines "choice" as "the power or opportunity of choosing." In His Sermon on the Mount, Jesus said, *You cannot serve two masters...you will hate one and love the other, or else the other way around.* [8] He then addresses those issues which concern all of us. With typical clarity, He assures us that our Heavenly Father is already aware of what we need. *He will give them to you if you give Him first place in your life.* [9]

Choices are a critical issue. They are the foundation of our relationship with Christ. Choices, or lack of them, reflect basic attitudes—how we view our relationship with God, ourselves and others.

The choice of who controls the direction you plan for your life, along with your relationship with your Heavenly Father, is an early essential. You feel that you are a good person. You really do try to do the right thing. After all, you have never killed nor stolen. Unfortunately, *no one is good—no one in all the world is innocent.* [10] Sin is not necessarily the commission of some terrible act. It is much simpler. *Knowing what is right to do and then not doing it is sin.* [11] Yet even with this sweeping indictment, He calls for our honesty and assures *if we confess our sins to Him, He can be depended on to forgive us and to cleanse us from every wrong.* [12] With our simple and sincere act of repentance, *God says he will accept and acquit us—declare us 'not guilty'—if we trust Jesus Christ to take away our sins.* [13]

The day I made the conscious decision to become a pilot did not automatically make me one. I had to address many issues, such as where and when I would take my training, how I would finance the costs, and what sacrifices I would be willing to make. I addressed the daily choices required by training, and many, many others. But because my goal was clear, all decisions I made supported the ultimate goal I had set. This same principle applies to your life and the choices you must begin to make.

You are beginning to rebuild a structure which may have been neglected for years. Often, because of emotional pain, we desire the "quick fix," an instant solution. However, it probably took months or years to arrive where you are now. It is going to take consistent action and choices to turn your life around. You have chosen to put Christ first in your life, but now other choices will be presented. You must address each one.

Personally, these implications were formidable. By training, I have always planned ahead, thinking out courses of action and possible alternatives. But I found the enemy used this in an attempt to overwhelm me. The sheer magnitude of the crisis alone was almost more than I could cope with. Now the requirement to face added decisions was enough to make me crash and burn.

Checklists used on the flight deck are developed to perfection through the experience of thousands of flight hours. They are designed to address crisis quickly and efficiently. We too have a checklist that omits nothing. Two thousand years ago, as He sat on the hillside speaking to the vast sea of expectant faces, He must have seen my face and knew my fear. *Don't be anxious about tomorrow. God will take care of your tomorrow too. Live one day at a time.* [14]

Paul may not have been a pilot, but he certainly understood the "crew concept." *Keep your eyes on Jesus, your [captain] and instructor.* [15] The Captain isn't going anywhere—he is along for the ride with you. He will *never fail you nor forsake you.* [16] *If you want to keep from becoming faint hearted and weary, think about his patience as sinful men did such terrible things to him.* [17] Next, *You can trust God to keep the [problem] from becoming [so big you can't handle it.] He will show you how to escape!* [18] Finally, *Don't worry about anything; instead pray...if you do this you will experience God's peace.* [19]

Now if that's not a formula for success, I've never read one. Paraphrased it reads, "Watch cappy and learn! He's with you for the duration of the flight (your life)! He's got all the experience and passed all tests! Now relax! He's got this whole mess so scoped out that it's just a matter of how smooth the landing will be, not whether or not we will land."

Right now, your goal is to gain insight and guidance to resolving areas of hurt. Having made certain the basic priorities are correct, you can now move confidently forward with the many other issues of your life. You have prepared a solid foundation upon which to build those decisions.

Some choices you face may involve holding grudges versus forgiveness. Others may deal with motives. Are you seeking only relief or are you really wanting to meet Christ? Are you just trying to *squirm out of our problem* [20] or are you sincerely willing to let God mold your life in His character and likeness? You may have to resolve the issue of blame— blaming others instead of accepting responsibility for your own action or inaction. No one could anticipate the many areas which you may face.

But how do I know what to do? What does God really want from me?

There is only one source on which you can rely. *If you want to know what God wants you to do, ask Him, and He will gladly tell you, for He is always ready to give a bountiful supply of wisdom to all who ask Him...but when you ask Him, be sure that you really expect Him to tell you...* [21] *...If you want better insight and discernment, and are searching for them as you would for lost money or hidden treasure, then wisdom will be given to you...for the Lord grants wisdom!* [22]

One area of emotional pain was realizing that necessary choices were either compromised or avoided. Because my priorities were questionable at best, my foundation was a "house of cards." My decisions were flawed. When memories came flooding back to my mind, the enemy used them to inflict emotional pain, driving me lower and lower. I finally realized I had a choice to make. God had forgiven me! If I believed Him, I stood before him blameless. Now, was I going to forgive myself? The consequence of my actions were still there, but with His help, I was able to move on and allow Him to resolve the hurt.

A close friend, a new Christian, met a lovely lady. A relationship began to bloom. He felt there was a real possibility of falling in love with her. As the friendship grew, he wanted to be sure she would accept his commitment to Christ. He invited her to attend his church home. After doing so, she made it clear that she was not ready to accept his beliefs. He had arrived at a crossroad. He faced difficult choices. Torn between his love for the Lord and his new-found potential life partner, he faced the necessity of choosing one or the other. As we talked, his pain was obvious. "I'm just not sure I'm ready for this kind of choice."

My heart ached for him. I knew only too well what he was saying. I had not been ready to make the choices which were thrust upon me. Given the alternative, none of us will deliberately walk into an area requiring painful decisions. Yet it seems they always drop on us when we are most vulnerable. If I hit one finger with a hammer, I wish it had been another. It just might have handled the pain better. When pain lays its icy palm on us, we are never ready.

But that is where the difference begins. If our relationship with our Heavenly Father is intact, we have a *refuge and strength, a tested help in times of trouble.* [23] Our Leader will not allow us to skip parts of the checklist. Instead, He will gently guide us through the maze of our emotions, hurts, and confusion. *If you will only let me help you, if you will only obey...* [24] clearly reveal His requirements. We must WANT His help and OBEY His direction.

In January, 1976, a friend suffered the trauma of tragedy. When I wrote the poem below in an effort to help, little did I realize that ten years later, I would face the same crushing blow. The words were undoubtedly from the Author of Life, serving as a source of comfort. They are an exciting reminder. I had pushed His plan for my life into the background. Yet even then, His love and grace were at work in my life. I share these words, with the prayer that you too will make your choice to "fly again."

January 23, 1976

"Fear and hurt and loneliness, devastating though they be,
Are but the barriers that lock the heart and hide the soul.

But to each of us is given, by the One whose name is Love,
The wings of Faith and Hope to free the heart, reveal the soul.

But as it is in the course of things—as with the baby gull,
Unless he stretches and works and tries, the rushing wind
And thrill of the soar, will never be his no more.

Yet because we try to reach that place, where freedom from past is golden and pure,
Is no guarantee that along the way, the fear and the hurt, may not again try.

But if I keep trying and if I keep stretching, looking above and never behind,

---

One day I will soar in the sunlit silence of all of my hopes and all of my dreams."

Don't let circumstances dictate direction for life. Instead, let Him show you how to fly again. You can have your miracle. You do have a future with hopes and dreams. *I want you to trust me in your times of trouble, so I can rescue you, and you can give me glory.* [25]

You don't have to crash. There is no reason to be a casualty. You have a choice. Exercise it! *Don't be upset. EXPECT GOD TO ACT!* [26]

If you are willing to make the right choices, don't worry about a parachute!

References

1   Galatians 6:7

2   Psalms 62:12

3   Matthew 12:36-37

4   James 1:6-8

5   John 10:10

6   I Kings 18:21

7   Joshua 24:15

8   Matthew 6:24

9   Matthew 6:33

10   Romans 3:10 and Psalms 14:3

11   James 4:17

12   I John 1:9

13   Romans 3:22

14   Matthew 6:34

15   Hebrews 12:2

16   Hebrews 13:5

17   Hebrews 12:3

18   I Corinthians 10:13

19   Philippians 4:6-7

20   James 1:4

21   James 1:5-6

22   Proverbs 2:3-6

23   Psalms 46:1

24   Isaiah 1:19

25   Psalms 50:14

26   Psalms 42:11

In A Crunch OR
Going To Crunch?

Chapter 5

There AIN'T
No Parachutes

Captain John Sherman* was a good pilot. His neatly trimmed salt and pepper hair, hat at a precise angle, and a spring in his determined stride left no doubt this man knew who he was. For those who cared to check further, the carefully groomed uniform, John's steady gaze, and quiet confidence all stated this man left nothing to chance. He knew his destination and knew he would get there.

Whenever passengers got off his flight, they were always smiling. They smiled because John had the ability to win their trust. When they trusted him, they relaxed. He made certain they enjoyed themselves. He went the extra mile to make sure they remembered his flights.

Early that morning, John and his crew had left San Antonio on their way to the East coast, four stops later. At the third stop, in his usually efficient manner, he obtained the flight papers and checked destination weather. As departure time arrived, checklists were run, push-back was accomplished, and engines were started. During taxi out, numbers were calculated for takeoff speeds. Preps for takeoff were finalized. With the words, "Cleared for takeoff," John slid the

(*The names and places have been changed, but the facts are true and accurate.)

throttles of his Boeing 727 forward to takeoff thrust and released the brakes.

The 727 rushed swiftly down the runway to lift off. The gear was quickly tucked away and flaps retracted as the airspeed built quickly past 200 toward target climb speed of 250 knots. Everything went smoothly, just the way John expected; anything else was unacceptable by his crew.

As the flight passed 17,000 feet, suddenly the aircraft shuddered violently as an explosion ripped deep in her heart. Simultaneously, engine and wheel well fire warning bells sounded, engine failure lights illuminated, and hydraulic quantities dropped to zero as warning lights blinked ominously on. Cabin depressurization horns joined the clamorous din warning of impending doom. The normally graceful ship yawed angrily to the right as if trying to shake off this unfamiliar and unwelcome intrusion, as number three engine quit running.

John and his crew fought valiantly to regain control. With no hydraulics, flight control responses were drastically reduced, providing only a sluggish return to normality. Because of cabin pressurization loss, quick donning of bulky oxygen masks required to sustain life further complicated the swift actions required. In-flight fire fighting procedures were accomplished to eliminate fire, the most feared of all in-flight emergencies. John had two, one on number three engine and one in the right wheel well. Further adjustments to flight controls and trim were necessary to compensate for the loss of number three engine.

Cabin depressurization normally requires an emergency descent to lower altitudes, but this maneuver strains a normal airframe, let alone one that had just experienced an explosion. In John's normally efficient manner, he had been aware of a crew member riding in the passenger cabin. While his crew continued through the maze of emergency checklists, John called the extra man to the front and instructed him to determine the extent of damage, structural integrity, and the location of the explosion. Meanwhile, terrified passengers were staring in horror at a hole the size of a barn door that had been blown in the right wing. They were looking through the wing at the ground far below.

With structural integrity established, John managed the descent to an altitude at which oxygen was no longer required for either crew or passengers. Air Traffic Control guided the flight by the most direct route back to the airfield. All other traffic was diverted to give priority to the crippled plane. As the aircraft touched down in a picture-perfect landing, passengers broke into spontaneous applause and cheers. As usual, they were smiling as they left. They would never forget John Sherman and his crew.

A few days after his harrowing experience, I had the opportunity to speak with John. Naturally, I was curious about his feelings during such a critical time. I asked him to describe the experience.

With characteristic humor he observed, "Well, I guess you can say we were 'bout as busy as cat's paws on a hot tin roof." Not satisfied, I pressed for honesty. What had been his reaction at the moment this was happening to him? I will never forget his reply.

After a moment of reflection, his answer was amazingly direct. "I wanted out! But since we didn't have chutes, we just had to dig ourselves out."

Captain John Sherman, the captain's Captain—the man whose bearing and calm blue eyes instilled confidence in even the rookie flier, was admitting that he had been afraid, had almost been overwhelmed, and didn't want to be there. He wanted out! But he had to wait! Wait while damage was assessed. Wait until he could get to a lower altitude. Wait until each checklist had been meticulously followed to the last detail. Wait for ATC to guide him safely back to the airfield. Wait until he was safely on the ground. Just WAIT!

We are never prepared when tragedy strikes. There is always the unspoken expectation that "it won't happen to me," but without warning we find ourselves immersed in pain and suffering. Bewildered, we always ask, "Why?"

Deep within each person is the necessity to understand what is happening, to find some reason that justifies the excruciating agony which rips at the fabric of life. So often, when the need for answers and reason is most urgent, it seems suddenly there is a vacuum which isolates us from friends and family. Even more devastating, our Heavenly Father seems to have gone on vacation. Isolation feels total.

We become excited when we see His hand of blessing. We understand because, after all, He loves us! But then we are suddenly catapulted into tragedy, blue skies turn into threatening storms, the calm waters into raging seas, and *floods of sorrow pour upon me like a thundering cataract.* [1] Then we are forced to wait, simply wait with no reason or answer forthcoming to satisfy our need for rationale. These times of pain-filled waiting and isolation, given what we know and understand about our Heavenly Father, are extremely difficult for us to reconcile.

The vivid memory remains of sleepless nights. I struggled to maintain a semblance of equilibrium, to survive the pain while I searched for answers. I prayed that somehow with the sun's first rays, relief would come. Falling into exhausted sleep, I would wake minutes later because the crushing thoughts of loneliness and rejection would creep through the subconscious and jar the mind into wakefulness and bitter recall. The mental gymnastics to resolve issues, listening late into the night to the television host assuring that God was there, were without any practical evidence that brought relief to me. All served to accentuate the vacuum of waiting in which I found myself enclosed. *Lord, WHY are you standing aloof and far away? WHY do you hide when I need you the most?* [2] *My mind is filled with apprehension and with gloom...I am worn out with pain; every night my pillow is wet with tears.* [3]

I struggled hard with the "why" of waiting to find plausible explanations. The final conclusion can be only this. The true reason for God's silence during our times of anguish and waiting will remain a mystery. But He does not leave us without clues.

The Apostle John relates a poignant story of waiting.[4] One day, tragedy struck a family Jesus loved, a family that was an intimate part of his life. It was this family who opened their home to provide a place to which Jesus could escape and just "be at home," away from the noise and demands of the crowd.

One day, a messenger arrived and announced to Jesus, *Sir, your good friend is very, very sick.* The narrative relates that *He loved Martha, and her sister and Lazarus very much.* Yet, when He heard the news, Jesus made the <u>conscious decision</u>

to stay away for two days and *made no move to go to them.* Why, when with just a word, Jesus could have resolved the problem and hurt? Why would He deliberately, purposely, and knowingly choose to remain absent? He knew His absence would cause pain and cause his friends to question Him. Even his disciples could not understand, and in an effort to understand, they began to speculate as to the reason.

Was it because he did not care? No, in fact, when Jesus finally arrived at the tomb, we are told simply that He *wept*. Even Jewish leaders standing there observed, *see how much He loved him.* So the question becomes even more complex. **Why would Jesus remain absent** when He cared so much about Lazarus and knew that His absence would cause pain to those He loved?

Jesus answered that question directly. There is a higher purpose that you and I might not understand in our times of pain-filled waiting. *I, the Son of God, will receive glory from this situation.* Just as gold taken from the ground must be put in the fire to remove impurities and reveal its true character, our times of waiting are signs of His loving hand at work. This molding and shaping, this refining and polishing process of some quality of character has a purpose. He wants your life to reflect with pure clarity the divine nature of our caring and loving Father.

The pain of waiting can become so intense we begin to doubt the reality of His love. But *Christ came at just the right time and died for us who had no use for him. Even if we were good, we really wouldn't expect anyone to die for us—but God showed his great love for us by sending Christ to die for us while we were still sinners.* [5] Christ made a commitment to us long before we ever made one to Him. Now, because we accepted His act of sacrificial love, we can be assured of His commitment to us in our times of waiting, even when we don't feel His presence.

Imagine for a moment, standing at the grave side of loved ones. Torrents of grief threaten to overwhelm you. Suddenly, Jesus walks up, and with a few words, restores that loved one to you. Instead of the clammy coldness of death, you feel the warmth of their touch. They throw their arms around you, holding and comforting, assuring that everything is O.K. The absolute joy would be indescribable.

They were His dearest friends. But because He was preparing them for something greater, He deliberately remained absent. Even though He had chosen to remain where He was for two full days, He was still in charge, in control of every detail of the situation.

But couldn't this grief and hurt been avoided?

Yes. But the lesson He wanted to teach and the refining process He was trying to accomplish would not be completed. Greatness is never awarded. It is always earned— earned on the battlefield through adversity, by men and women who dared to step beyond themselves to become the exception. In this time of waiting, you and I are given the opportunity to be a part of His purpose and plan.

This tender story shows He will act—the night will always end. When trapped in the vacuum of waiting, the enemy will try to convince us this is the end, there is no future or hope, that we will never be happy or fulfilled again. But that is not God's plan. *Weeping may go on all night, but in the morning there is joy.* [6] Just as surely as there is a night of waiting, there is going to come the dawn of a new day, a new time in which Jesus will step forward and end the time of waiting.

Jesus stood before the tomb, tears streaming down His face, not out of sorrow for Lazarus, but because He cared about the hurting emotions of the ones He loved. He did not allow pain because He was insensitive or uncaring. As soon as the waiting had accomplished its goal, He did not delay another moment. First, He simply thanked God for hearing Him, then with a shout that must have reverberated across the valley, He shouted, *Lazarus, come out!*

As stunned observers watched, Lazarus came walking out of the tomb. Jesus turned to the group and simply said, *Let him go.* The trial was over, the goals accomplished. It was now time to release the burden of pain, to end the stressful time of waiting, to set His suffering child free. You must never doubt, when the time is right and perfect, Jesus will act in your behalf. For *we know that all that happens to us is working for our good if we love God and are fitting into His plans.* [7]

I cannot count the many nights I lay awake or paced through my home, unable to sleep, praying that God would somehow relieve the hurt. Days stacked into weeks, weeks stretched into months as I sought answers. I will never forget the intense struggle late one night as I fought my feelings of rejection and loneliness. Adding to the despair, a very dear friend had visited me several weeks earlier. Since leaving, I had not heard a single word from her. As I prayed, I knew I was losing control of my emotions. The hours of pain-filled waiting were so intense I was losing the perspective I needed to see the reality of His loving involvement in my life instead of the circumstance.

Knowing I needed help, I called my Dad on the phone and shared my struggle with him. He began to remind me how special I was to God, how much He loved and cared for me, and how I was not trusting Him to handle the situation. As always, he started sharing the Word, *The Lord is close to those whose hearts are breaking...* [8] *commit everything you do to the Lord. Trust Him to help you do it and He will.* [9] Finally he commented, "Son, I don't know how, but God is going to work everything out—just hang in there."

While he was talking, I just could not shake the terrible cloud of depression. I asked him to pray. As he began, I told God again, "I WILL trust You no matter what or how I feel." I reminded Him how badly I was hurting. I asked Him specifically why I had not heard from my friend. As I mentioned her name in prayer, the words of the psalmist flashed into my mind, *I want you to trust me in your times of trouble, so I can rescue you, and you can give me glory...* [10]

At that precise moment, the other line on my phone rang. I answered the phone and the gentle voice of my friend came reassuringly across the line. It was midnight. She had no idea of the pain I was in. But God knew how deeply I was hurting, how much I missed her, and at the perfect and most beautiful moment, He acted. Within ten minutes after the call was complete, I was asleep. It is so beautiful and timely when He acts on our behalf and provides the miracle we need.

Acts 27 relates the exciting story of part of Paul's trip to Rome. Because it had encountered stiff winds and heavy seas, the ship had stopped at the small port of Fair Havens. As the trip was about to commence, Paul warned there was trouble ahead. But logical reasons by the captain and owners convinced the crew to press on. Soon, the ship was trapped in a *terrible storm [which] raged unabated many days, until at last all hope was gone.* [11] They knew they were losing it, that they were going to sink. But in the middle of the chaos and fear, Paul called the men and crew together. As he spoke, he said, *Cheer up! Not one of us will lose our lives, even though the ship will go down—for last night an angel of God to whom I belong... stood beside me and said, 'Don't be afraid!'* [12]

Paul and the crew were immersed in a struggle for their very lives. All hope was gone. They were trapped in the agony of waiting, not knowing the outcome of their fate. Yet in the middle of the uncertainty, fear, and hunger, Paul had managed a good night's sleep. He had been given peace in the middle of the storm. Jesus said, *I am leaving you with a gift—PEACE of mind and heart! And the peace I give isn't fragile like the peace the world gives. So don't be troubled or afraid.* [13]

When you find yourself trapped in the agony of waiting, remember:

- God loves you, and cares deeply about your hurt.

- He is in charge of your life. *I know the plans I have for you...* [14]

- He has a design in your adversity—you have the opportunity to become the exception.

- He is working everything out for your good.

- He WILL act—your time of waiting WILL end.

- There is PEACE in the middle of the storm.

There AIN'T
No Parachutes

This waiting time should be a time of self-examination for growth and for becoming intimately acquainted with your Lord. But there is also the "other choice," the alternative, if allowed.

King Saul was in the second year of his reign as king. God had rewarded his trust and obedience with outstanding victories in battle, using only a handful of men, against the enemies of Israel. One day, in retaliation, the Philistines gathered a *mighty army. When the men of Israel saw the vast mass of enemy troops, they lost their nerve entirely and tried to hide in caves, thickets, coverts, among the rocks, and even in tombs and cisterns.* [15] Saul was faced with such mass desertion of his troops he became very concerned.

Saul had contacted Samuel, the prophet of God. Samuel had told Saul to WAIT for seven days and he would come. As the days wore on, more and more troops disappeared. Saul stood on the hill, looking out over the mighty forces which had gathered against his dwindling band, and waiting became a torment. The pressure became so great that even another moment was too much—Saul just couldn't wait; he had to act. He acted in panic!

As the days and weeks of waiting march slowly on, the pressures begin to build. The urge to understand and make sense of what is happening, to reassure ourselves that something is being done on our behalf, continue to exert inner pressures which demand we do something! Just waiting makes us feel so vulnerable, so open, and so alone. Because of the fear, "tunnel vision" [16] sets in and we only see our isolation and our circumstance, instead of concentrating on His ability to intervene in any circumstance. Trust in our Heavenly Father is dissipated, and eventually, we wrench control out of His hands to reassert our own will. We act foolishly without God's loving hand of guidance in our life. With this forced deviation, we actually delay His plan and our time of waiting becomes even longer.

Even as Saul was in the act of refusing to wait a moment longer, Samuel arrived. The old prophet was visibly upset, for he knew the consequence of Saul's panic. It had revealed a flaw in the character of Saul, an insensitivity to God's plan and timing. In his rush to relieve the panic which he felt in his waiting time, Saul lost his kingdom. *You have disobeyed the commandment of the Lord—He was planning to make you and your descendants kings of Israel forever, but now your dynasty must end.* [17]

Saul's panic reached the boiling point just moments before God's perfect timing for resolution of the problem. When the panic comes, the times when you wonder if you can stand the hurt and pain a moment longer, when you become so restless and the urge to do something becomes irresistible, STOP! Those feelings of panic are a sign that God's timing for resolution of your problem is drawing to a close. They are His voice, warning not to act foolishly and risk the handiwork He has already accomplished. They are His assurance to you that He is still in control and is working out every detail in your best interest.

You have the choice, to either view your circumstance with all its negative connotations, or to *keep your eyes on Jesus, your leader and instructor.* [18] The time has come to realize *there is no longer any room for doubt..for there is no question that he will do what he says.* [19]

Why do you have to wait—waiting the pain-filled hours when nothing makes sense, when answers do not seem to be coming? I do not know, but one thing is certain, He does! And when His timing is right, He will act. Today, you may feel you are suspended in a timeless capsule of uncertainty with heavy chains pulling you further down each day. But remember, the day will come when your Father will say, "Enough is enough!"

Mounted on the cherubim, He [will speed] swiftly to [your] aid with wings of wind. He enshrouded Himself with darkness, veiling His approach with dense clouds dark as murky waters. [But] suddenly the brilliance of His presence [will break] through the clouds with lightning and a mighty storm of hail—the God above all gods has spoken—He [will reach] down from heaven and [take you] and draw [you] out of [your] great trial. He [will] rescue [you] from deep waters.[20] He [will lift you] out of the pit of despair, out from the bog and the mire, and set [your] feet on a hard, firm path and steady [you] as [you] walked along. He has given [you] a new song to sing, of praises to our God. Now many will hear the glorious things He did for [you], and stand in awe before the Lord, and put their trust in Him. [21] Rest in the Lord; wait patiently for Him to act.. Stop your anger! Turn off your wrath. Don't fret and worry—it only leads to harm.. don't be impatient for the Lord to act! Keep traveling steadily along His pathway and in due season He will honor you with every blessing... [22]

You don't need a parachute, but you've got to get past the fear!

References

1   Psalms 42:7

2   Psalms 10:1

3   Psalms 6:3,6

4   John 11

5   Romans 5:6-8

6   Psalms 30:5

7   Romans 8:28

8   Psalms 34:18

9   Psalms 37:5

10 Psalms 50:14

11 Acts 27:20

12 Acts 27:22-23

13 John 14:27

14 Jeremiah 29:11

15 I Samuel 13:6

16 A condition which destroys peripheral vision and allows one
    to see only a very narrow field of concentrated vision.

17 I Samuel 13:13-14

18 Hebrews 12:2

19 Hebrews 10:23

20 Psalms 18:10-16

21 Psalms 40:2-3

22 Psalms 37:7-8,34

Chapter 6

I'm Not Paranoid. She IS Out To Get Me!

Tonight, "SHE" was Mother Nature. It's not nice to fool Mother Nature! We didn't know who had tried to fool her, but she was in a foul mood. Her temper tantrums had already nearly destroyed one city in Ohio. Now in the early morning hours, she was showing no signs of being placated.

My flight had left Chicago's O'Hare Airport enroute to Kansas City International. As we approached Kansas City, our radar painted a bleak picture. A thunderstorm line west of the city stretched to the southwest as far as our radar could see, over 200 miles away. Conferring with the Air Traffic Control Center did nothing to change our discomfort. Their radar scope saw miles beyond ours and they could not see the end of the line either.

Usually, these lines have breaks, "soft" spots between the thunderstorm cells through which braver souls can venture. Not this one. The cells were close together, overlapping each other like warriors linking arms, marching mercilessly eastward, daring anything to stand in their way.

After our stop in Kansas City, we rolled slowly toward the runway. We turned to give our radar a better view of the skies while we searched for clues on the best departure route. With the help of Center we finally decided to stay east of the line as we headed south. However, this would necessitate crossing the line somewhere. We were hoping we would find something more encouraging than we faced locally.

Takeoff and climbout were uneventful. As we made our tentative way southward the skies to the west provided a constant kaleidoscopic display of fireworks as Mother Nature did her best to impress us. As far as I was concerned, she was doing a great job. I just wanted to go home and get in bed.

With each spectacular flash of lightning, we could see illuminated the great canyons created by the thunderheads towering far above us. We felt infinitesimally small and vulnerable. Time was running out; somewhere, somehow, we had to pass through the line. To the west of the line lay relative calm with clear sailing and smooth air to our destination.

An eastbound flight had just come through the line only a few minutes earlier. The turbulence was described as "light to moderate" in their location. That sounded fine to us. We had no desire to pioneer new routes of discovery that night. We asked Center to vector us to the same area. As we neared the line, it looked passable on our radar as well. However, we cautioned the cabin crew to remain in their seats with belts on. We slowed to turbulent air penetration speed just in case. The lightning was almost continuous, showing the wall of clouds ahead. Suddenly, we were in it.

With a violent shudder we encountered the first wave of turbulence. "Light to moderate" had suddenly turned to "severe." Under normal flight conditions, any turn is limited to a maximum bank of 30 degrees. We now found ourselves fighting just to maintain control as bank angles approached

45 degrees, first in one direction and then the other. The buffeting became so severe we actually encountered the phenomena of "eyeball bounce," [1] making it almost impossible to read our instruments. Rain slashed the windshield with the intensity of a thousand marbles, threatening to break it at any moment. In one instant, we were slammed down into the seat making it impossible to raise our arms, the next, jerked painfully into the shoulder harnesses.

For the first time, I felt we would not survive. Our aircraft would surely be torn apart by the violence of the storm. In the next moments we would be gone, a mere headline to be read in tomorrow morning's paper, detailing the crash with loss of all lives on board. I was terrified yet strangely objective, clinically observing what I felt was about to happen. Though emotionally resigned, I was still physically occupied with making it through to the calm on the other side of the storm.

Then, just as suddenly as it had engulfed us, we were out of the storm. We sat there in stunned silence, mechanically going through the routine of flying the airplane, immersed in our own private and thankful thoughts. A short while later we landed at our destination.

The impact of what we had encountered continued to grow over the next hours and days. As I began to anticipate my next flight assignment, for the first time ever I experienced a high degree of anxiety. I found myself carefully scrutinizing weather reports, trying to determine what the weather would be when I was next assigned to fly. One day I had to ride as a passenger to the next flight assignment. The weather was less than perfect but similar to that in which I had flown hundreds of times before. When we encountered some light turbulence, I realized I was gripping the arm rest so hard that my muscles were cramping. I was actually sweating. The thrill of flying I had once experienced was gone.

Around the aviation industry there is an old saying, "There are old pilots, and there are bold pilots, but there are no old, bold pilots." This epitomizes the normally conservative outlook most pilots employ. Fear, on the other hand, is destructive, inhibiting creative and intelligent responses to critical events which may present themselves. Fear can cause a man to "freeze," to become so immobile he cannot function within the crew structure. I was for the first time fearful of the flight environment. The haunting specter of losing my career raised its ugly head. This problem required me to analyze and then address this critical issue.

Fear of real danger in real situations is healthy. However, the fear and anxiety which come from motivations or emotions not based in reality, are destructive. The fear of feeling worthless which possibly results from rejection by someone you trusted, is just such a fear.

Fear is a malfunction. During normal flight, all systems of the aircraft function normally. But when a system fails, the exhilaration of flight is replaced with concern and fear. When tragedy touches a normally functioning life, the protective devices built into us by our Creator suddenly shut down in response. The self-reliant human system becomes vulnerable. The instinct of "self-preservation" takes over as man initiates any step necessary to defend himself. This mechanism can take many forms, ranging from withdrawal and silence to belligerence and criticism. But no matter what form, it all boils down to the same thing, the desire for invulnerability.

Every instinct in man warns, "Protect yourself—hide your weakness." During social encounters, people play roles designed to keep others at arm's length. Never get too close to be hurt. Business always tries to negotiate from a "position of strength" to gain the advantage. If mistakes are made, we rarely hear the admission, "I was wrong!" Instead we bluff and bluster, trying to cover and hide our vulnerability.

Fear must have an object. When personal tragedy strikes, the object of fear becomes personal: fear of the circumstance in which we are immersed, fear of loneliness because of a lost relationship, fear to trust because someone betrayed us, leaving us raw and bleeding emotionally, fear of people and their demands as we seek their approval, or fear of future failure because of past mistakes. These and more haunt many of us, causing a malfunction in God's normal design for our lives.

Fear causes us to generate a false front. We bluff to hide our real self and our weaknesses. Because of this lack of honesty, relationships are clouded, wrought with the uncertainty that accompanies the "games" we hide behind. Our relationship with God suffers. We do not trust and commit ourselves to His loving guidance. Fear clouds our minds, hindering us from being useful and productive, from thinking creatively and responsively. Fear prevents us from reaching goals. Its obsessiveness takes precedence as the survival instinct leaves no time for the business of living.

Fear now takes on a new dimension, becoming a spiritual problem. Just as darkness is the absence of light, so fear and anxiety are the absence of faith. Faith is *the confident assurance that something we want is going to happen. It is the certainty that what we hope for is waiting for us, even though we cannot see it up ahead.* [2] Fear is worry with panic!

Faith is the opposite of the false front, the clouded thinking, the doubtful relationship, the faltering goals, and the feelings of panic in crisis. That is why *you can never please God without faith, without depending on Him.* [3] Contrast this picture of wavering man, to that of a Man led to a place called Calvary. There between two thieves, naked and alone, God made Himself vulnerable to the whole world in the person of Jesus Christ.

I will never forget a scene I witnessed. An older, single lady missionary had been invited to speak to a group of professionals. As she began to speak, it was apparent she was no great orator. But with a sensitivity gained through her relationship with Christ, she began to share not her victories, but her fears, failures, and vulnerability to cultures, situations, and people. She described the pain of loneliness in a strange land, the desire for companionship when her only companions were the strange sounds in the night from the jungle. She shared the frustration of failure under the duress of severe circumstances in a new and strange land. Even in these experiences, she shared how His loving hand touched lives even through what she perceived as failure.

When she had finished, there was not a dry eye. Each person there had identified with her openness and vulnerability and was instinctively drawn to her. She had graphically demonstrated that God's love is most understood at this point of vulnerability.

Apprehension and dread drain us of our energy, rob us of precious time, and destroy our creative interface with God, others, and even ourselves. When our minds are occupied with fear and worry, our energy is diverted to nonproductive activity and our thoughts distracted from trusting our Heavenly Father. *A doubtful mind will be as unsettled as a wave of the sea that is driven and tossed by the wind, and every decision you then make will be uncertain, as you turn first this way, and then that.* [4]

Jesus stood on the slopes one day and addressed this very issue. He cautioned that worry over "things" [5] came about because of our warped sense of values (vs. 25), because of our incorrect priorities in life (vs. 28-29), and because of a wavering sense of relationship with our Father (vs. 31-33). When we view our own situations and the mistakes we make, we worry. The relationships we develop, with all the potential for love and acceptance or rejection and disillusionment, create anxiety. We worry that people will hurt us through betrayal of our emotions so we become competitive and hard, destroying our openness and sensitivity. If this worry takes root, it becomes resentment and destroys our peace of mind, creating panic and confusion. *I came so close to the edge of the cliff! My feet were slipping and I was almost gone. For I was envious of the prosperity of the proud and wicked.* [6] *When I saw this, what turmoil filled my heart! I saw myself so stupid and so ignorant... But even so, You loved me!* [7] In spite of our mistakes, God provides an alternative to the crippling grip of fear and anxiety. *I get as close to Him as I can! I have CHOSEN Him... He rescues me.* [8]

After that turbulent flight, I worked hard to overcome the fear which clutched me in its tentacles. With each subsequent flight, I found certain actions, mind sets, and attitudes were required to help me regain my original joy of flying. As I applied these insights, slowly the fear was conquered and laid to rest.

How can we overcome our fear? Can we ever again slip the bonds of earth and thrill to soaring flight once again? Can we ever again be free of the crippling anxiety that drains emotions, robs us of precious time, precludes creative living, and deadens relationships?

The only answer that counts is the one He has given. *My purpose is to give life in ALL ITS FULLNESS.* [9]

So how do we find it?

References

1   A condition when the body is shaken so violently that the eyeballs literally bounce in their sockets, causing difficulty in focusing on or reading instruments.

2   Hebrews 11:1

3   Hebrews 11:6

4   James 1:6-7

5   Matthew 25:25-34

6   Psalms 73:2-3

7   Psalms 73:21-22

8   Psalms 73:28

9   John 10:10

I'm Not Paranoid. She
IS Out To Get Me!

81

Chapter 7

Just One Big Simulator!

Pat was my First Officer. An F-16 fighter pilot fresh out of the Air Force, he exuded the confidence so typical of his breed. He was good and knew it. If he weren't, he wouldn't last long in aerial combat.

He was new to the multi-engine environment of large commercial jetliners. He was thrilled with his new job and applied himself to every task; he was a pleasure to fly with. If something new came up, he was a quick study and didn't make the same mistake twice.

It was our turn for takeoff. The long runway at Denver stretched out in front of the windshield. The day was perfect; to the west, the Rockies appeared close enough to touch. It was Pat's leg to fly.

We rolled down the runway and at the perfect moment, lifted the nose and became airborne. He called for "gear up." Suddenly, the calm was shattered. The computerized voice warning system called, "WINDSHEAR, WINDSHEAR!" He slammed the throttles to the firewall as I began to call out his flight path. He was fighting for our survival.

"Altitude 300 feet. Sink 200 down. Altitude 250 feet. Sink 400 down. Airspeed decreasing. Altitude 200 feet. Sink 1000 down."

While Pat struggled to keep our aircraft airborne, I watched our deteriorating flight path. If something didn't happen soon, we would crash! Even with the throttles full forward, I pressed against them, hoping somehow to squeeze just a little extra power from the engines.

I continued the call outs.

"Sink 1000 down. Altitude 100 feet. Airspeed decreasing. Sink 800 down. Altitude 75 feet."

Out of the corner of my eye, I could see the ground rushing by just below us. Desperate, I made the call outs louder.

"Altitude 50 feet. Sink 500 down."

I could hear Pat pleading, "Come on, baby. Fly!" He was desperately nursing the aircraft on the fine edge between stall and sinking into the ground.

It was to no avail. Suddenly, with a grinding crash, the tail struck the ground, then the main fuselage. We were slammed back and forth as the crippled aircraft skidded across the ground. Then the cockpit went black.

The silence was deafening. I turned to look at Pat. It was obvious he was shaken, staring straight ahead as if in a trance. Both of us realized the consequences if this had been real.

Our instructor broke the spell. "O.K.! Let's try that again!"

You see, we were in the simulator.

Most major airlines have simulators. These computerized marvels with their visual graphics simulate every phase of the flight environment, including sight, sound, and motion. For all practical purposes, you are in the aircraft and flying. It is the exact duplicate of the cockpit. Everything that can go wrong will go wrong in the simulator for this is the place pilots are taught to hone their skills and to deal with emergencies. The only thing you can't do in the simulator is kill yourself. You're on the ground, in a building, inside a box called a simulator. Here, you can safely practice maneuvers and flight emergencies that would be impossible in flight without risking lives.

With the push of a button the instructor "fixed" our aircraft and positioned us back on the end of the runway. He pointed out the mistakes we had made, indicated how it should have been handled, and then said to me, "O.K., it's your turn in the hot seat."

Believe me, I had learned from Pat's mistakes. As we began our takeoff roll, every muscle in my body was tense in anticipation. Even though this was another windshear profile, it would be different from the one Pat encountered. After rotation, I called for gear up. For the first 500 feet, everything seemed normal. Then things began to unravel.

Pat now provided the call outs. I struggled to maintain control, doing my best to recall the instructor's advice. The aircraft bucked near stall one second, then tried to roll over on her back the next. Slowly but surely, we sank closer and closer to the ground, teetering on the edge of oblivion. Then, just as suddenly as we had been hit, Mother Nature released her hold and the aircraft began to climb skyward. I was sweating!

We had made it! Not because I was better than Pat, but because of reinforced training that helped us perform at a higher level of skill as a crew. The simulator helps provide the greatest possible safety.

In the simulator, pilots expect to encounter problems. They don't necessarily enjoy this annual ritual, but realize its necessity. Their lives and those of their passengers depend on their developed skills.

Life is no different. *Here on earth you will have many trials and sorrows...* [1] Trials are not a once-in-a-lifetime happening; they are an ongoing process. You are expected to *...[put] into practice all you learned...* [2] This is the only way we can refine our lives so they will best reflect our Heavenly Father. We should *...rejoice when we run into problems and trials.. they help us learn patience. Patience develops strength of character.. helps us trust God more.. until finally our hope and faith are strong and steady.* [3]

The only reason you would get on an airplane is because you have faith in the pilot's ability. Of course, it also helps to realize that he is in the aircraft, too.

Faith and hope help us anchor ourselves to God. They give us strength when ours are gone and stimulates our inner transformation. In other words, we stop believing IN God and start BELIEVING GOD—a big difference! Now *there is no longer any room for doubt.. for there is no question that He will do what He says.* [4]

Life is God's simulator!

When He first created us and provided the Garden of Eden, He wanted our fellowship and companionship. Sin destroyed that. His perspective is eternal; He knows our days are numbered and quickly disappear. He has built the very best simulator possible to prepare us for the future. More than anything else, He wants to help us prepare for the biggest flight of our lives.

The wide, easy road just "goes with the flow," but the *Gateway to Life is small.. the road is narrow...* [5] when you choose to perfect your skills in the simulator. The first choice leads to heartbreak, the second to the happy and fulfilled life. It is a choice each of us must make.

You are the best! God has chosen you. You already know you can do it. Don't delay a moment longer. Get in the simulator and start this exciting challenge. Start the checklist and watch just how exciting life can become.

Are you ready? O.K., then let's go!

"Ladies and gentlemen, welcome aboard! Here's the checklist your Captain recommends. Practice hard and you will find life is exciting and good. Thanks for choosing to fly again!"

1. Let God love you.

Does that sound strange? Yet I repeatedly hear, "If I really serve God, He might ask me to..." and a personal fear is expressed. If God asks us to do something, we must either obey or disobey. If we are afraid to listen we might also be afraid to obey. This attitude reflects a lack of trust. If we do not trust Him, how can we say we love Him? Love and trust go hand in hand.

You *need have no fear of someone who loves us perfectly; His perfect love for us eliminates all dread of what He might do to us. If we are afraid.. it shows that we are not fully convinced that He really loves us.* [6] God gave His only Son to demonstrate His love for us long before we made any commitment to Him. Now we must trust Him enough to let Him love us.

2. Put your money (TRUST) where your mouth is.

The story is told of aviation's early barnstorming days when a young pilot would offer rides to the local residents. One day he landed at a particular farm. After the farmer had given both the pilot and his flimsy craft the once-over, he indicated he was quite sure this new contraption could not lift him into the air. After much persuasion, however, the young pilot convinced the farmer to ride with him. After the ride was over and both were safely back on the ground, the pilot gleefully pointed out that the plane had been quite capable of lifting both of them into the air. The old farmer showed his doubt with the comment, "Well son, I never really put my full weight down."

Either you trust your Father or you don't. Have you really "put your full weight" of trust in Him? *I want you to trust me in your times of trouble, so I can rescue you…* [7] A person convinced that his trust is well-founded *does not fear bad news, nor live in dread of what may happen. For he has settled in his mind that Jehovah will take care of him. That is why he is not afraid, but can calmly face…* [8] his fears and anxieties. Holding onto fear and doubt demonstrates a lack of trust in your Heavenly Father. How can any relationship progress without trust?

3. Face your fear.

I had to face my fear of turbulence to regain the freedom and joy of flight. You too must face your fear. *Let there be tears for the wrong things you have done. Let there be sorrow and sincere grief. Let there be sadness instead of laughter, and gloom instead of joy. Then…He will lift you up, encourage and help you.* [9] Don't try to sweep your fear under the rug. Pull it out and show it to God, accepting the responsibility and the consequence. Then, realize God has a plan for your life and allow Him to take control. He will! You will find that He ...*does not want you to be afraid...* [10] His abundant life, life at its fullest, can and will be yours.

4. STOP hurting yourself—STOP worrying.

Name one important thing you have changed because of worry. You can't! If for some reason you affected the outcome, it was because you took action, not because you sat and worried. *Stop your anger! Turn off your wrath. Don't fret and worry—it only leads to harm.* [11] Instead, turn to Him. *In my distress I prayed to the Lord and He answered me and rescued me. He is for me! How can I be afraid? What can mere man do to me? The Lord is on my side, He will help me.* [12]

5. Put God FIRST in your life.

Without this priority, everything else is out of whack. *Give Him first place in your life and live as He wants you to.* [13] He must be the "Captain" of your life.

6. Live TODAY.

We all have been told to "stop and smell the roses." Yet with each day that passes, we can observe people rushing head-long toward the future while failing to capture the opportunities of the present. *What's the use of worrying? What good does it do? Will it add a single day to your life? Of course not! And if worry can't even do such little things as that, what's the use of worrying over bigger things?* [14] Don't overload and crush today with concern and worry about tomorrow. *Don't be anxious about tomorrow. God will take care of your tomorrow too. Live one day at a time.* [15]

Stop and analyze your worries. Almost all are about something you anticipate in your future. You don't worry about the present because it is here; you are experiencing and living it.

The past is gone forever, etched in the granite of time. Nothing you can do will change one moment or failure of the past. Worrying and wishing you had not flown into a storm only distracts from today, killing all the wonderful potential you possess. What better way for Satan to neutralize your life! *No one, after putting his hand to the plow and looking back* (lets himself be distracted), *is fit for the kingdom of heaven.* [16] If you made mistakes, ask His forgiveness. Then leave them in His capable hands; never look back or be distracted by that worry again.

The future has not arrived. God has promised only the moment—TODAY! If Satan can distract you from the possibilities of today, neutralizing your potential with the plan God has for your life, then he has succeeded. Be careful, for he can make your worry seem justified. Paul understood this subtle yet devastating ability of the enemy when he wrote, *Satan can change himself into an angel of light, so it is no wonder his servants can... seem like godly ministers.* [17] Satan will use your worry about future possibilities until you are immobilized, choking any chance of God's loving involvement in your life today. You must constantly remind yourself, when your tomorrow arrives, He has promised He will take care of it, too. Make the most of today; it is yours to either creatively spend or tragically waste!

7. PRAY.

He is not a stopgap. He wants to be a companion and friend. When we need something, too often we try to make Him our "gopher." [18] I have found I must guard against this tendency. When I make Him my constant companion, my prayers are heard and answered so much more effectively. *You will find me when you seek me, IF you look for me in earnest.* [19] *Pray about everything...* [20]

Whenever we talk with a friend, there is an etiquette, an acceptable way of addressing them. The same applies when we talk with Him.

First, bring your petition. *Pray all the time. Ask God for anything in line with the Holy Spirit's wishes. Plead with him, reminding him of your needs, and keep praying earnestly.* [21] When you ask a favor of a friend, you spend time to communicate your need. The old "wham, bam, thanks" routine just does not endear us to the heart of any potential giver. God has feelings, too, and desires our honest interface with Him.

Second, offer your praise and thanks. *No matter what happens, always be thankful, for this is God's will for you...* [22] When you have given something to a friend, the least you expect is a little "thank you" for your trouble. An ungrateful heart smacks of selfishness. With selfishness in your life, priorities and motives come into question. Search your heart for hidden motives which may hinder your communion with Him.

Finally, bring yourself! God wants you to spend time alone with Him. Think about people you love. Is it natural to want to be away, absent, and silent? On the contrary, we desire to be near them, touch them, love them, talk with them. God wants the same from us. *Come boldly to the very throne of God, and stay there to receive His mercy and to find grace to help us in our times of need.* [23] God does not want to be a convenience, available only when we need Him. He wants our personal fellowship, companionship, praise, and worship.

He has promised to give you an inner peace which will guard your thoughts and emotions, relieving you from the fear and anxiety which robs of happiness. He is offering you freedom to press forward with your life and its exciting potential. He is giving you the chance to "FLY AGAIN!"

We have all observed individuals who seem happy only when they have something to worry about. Ask them how they are on a beautiful day. The probable response is, "Well, I THINK I'll make it with the Lord's help." Their answer belies the tone in their voice which anticipates having a miserable day. Above their heads they could easily have a sign reading, "Why pray when you can worry?"

The first seven steps in the simulator are good. However, unless you complete the final two, you will be just another person resigned to misery and failure. More than anything, you must desire to rid yourself of fear and worry.

STOP for a moment.

Tell God what is bothering you and what you want to do about it. Get real with Him. Don't try to phrase things in ethereal language like the minister. In your own words, tell God the deepest worries, hurts, anxieties, and desires of your heart. Ask the Holy Spirit to open your heart to His wonderful freedom. Ask Him to show you the possibilities in your life and let Him help you see how you can overcome. He has promised you *can do everything God asks [you] to with the help of Christ who gives [you] the strength and power.* [24]

Once you have turned it over to Him, now...

8. Start thinking RIGHT.

Throughout your life you have developed patterns of thought which you follow faithfully each day. Now for the first time, you must carefully check each thought as it enters your mind. If it is negative, falling into the old pattern, you must immediately put it in check. Instead, *fix your thoughts on what is true and good and right. Think about things that are pure and lovely, and dwell on the fine, good things in others. Think about all you can praise God for and be glad about.* [25] In other words, if a single negative thought, worry, or fear comes into your mind, kill it! Instead, start praising your Father for the good, the pure, and the lovely you can see, hear, and feel. *Resist the devil, and he will flee...* [26] You will find a wonderful transformation taking place. Very soon, you will begin to see other positive areas in your life for which you can thank Him.

Finally,

9. PRACTICE what you learn, and DEVELOP RIGHT PATTERNS.

It has been proven over and over in the cockpit. A person who has practiced certain actions, when confronted with crisis, will revert to those actions. I have often heard, "Well, if I know I am going to die, I'll just call on God and ask Him to forgive me." The evidence does not bear that out. During the investigation of a commercial airline crash, the final seconds on the flight recorder were played back. One of the pilots, very aware that the aircraft was crashing, was heard to be cursing, using God's name in vain.

Keep putting into practice all you learned—and the God of peace will be with you. [2] I did not learn to fly in one day. You

---

will not overcome fear and anxiety in one day. But as you faithfully **practice this new pattern of thought and action,** the God of the Universe, the Commander of all Heaven's armies, the Bright and Morning Star, and the Prince of Peace will walk by your side and no force on this earth will be *able to separate [you] from the Love of God.*[27]

"Visualization" is a concept used to help people succeed. Simply paint a detailed picture in your mind. Draw in all the details. Visualize how you would like to be, look, and act. Now start practicing that picture. Get a new hair style, dress up a notch, even shine the old shoes. When you step out, walk as if you were a successful, well off, business person. The minute your shoulders sag, put in a military brace.

What would your demeanor be if you turned and saw the President walking beside you? Well, you have Jesus by your side—act like it! Faithfully follow this "visual concept" you have developed of yourself with the help of the Holy Spirit. One morning you will wake to realize you are what you visualize. But just as this "visualization" will help, it can also hinder. Let all those negative, destructive, doubting thoughts pervade your thinking, and guess what you will be? Remember, *fix your thoughts on what is true and good and right…*[25] Practice. Practice. Practice.

A popular farewell of today is, "May the FORCE be with you." Well, you have far more than that. The next time you feel as if the whole world is crashing down around you, when your best friend betrays your trust, or when you wonder if God is still around to care, stop and think about Elisha's servant.

The King of Syria was at war with the King of Israel. One day the Syrian king called his commanders to plot an ambush.

But the Lord was listening and immediately told his prophet, Elisha, the time and the place. Elisha warned the King of Israel who promptly sent out a scout to check things out. Sure enough, it was just as the old prophet had said.

This happened several times, frustrating the Syrian king to no end. Being a good, paranoid king, he started accusing his own soldiers of treason. But one crafty old officer told the king, "Look, it's that old man, the Prophet Elisha who keeps squealing on us. He's the culprit!" The King of Syria finally had had enough, so he called in the tanks of the day (chariots) and the cavalry. Late one night he surrounded the city where the poor old prophet was staying.

Early the next morning Elisha's servant got up early to get breakfast ready for his master. Well, the poor lad nearly had a heart attack when he saw all the Syrian forces surrounding them. He ran up to Elisha to warn him, but the old prophet didn't even get excited. He simply stated, *Don't be afraid.. for our army is bigger than theirs.* [28] I'm sure the poor servant promptly concluded his master had finally gone over the edge.

But the old prophet gently looked toward heaven and prayed, *'Lord, open his eyes and let him see!' And the Lord opened the young man's eyes so he could see horses.. and chariots of fire everywhere upon the mountains.* Imagine the thrill and amazement which filled the heart of that young servant boy!

When you feel as though you are surrounded and pressured, you don't have a single guardian angel. Surrounding you are the forces of heaven with specific instructions from the Commander Himself, not to let anyone or anything cross the line which He has drawn. Nothing can come any closer to you than He permits. *I stand silently before the Lord, waiting for him to rescue me—He alone is my Rock, my rescuer, defense and fortress—why then should I be tense with fear when trouble comes? He is my refuge, a Rock where no enemy can reach me.* [29]

To paraphrase Teddy Roosevelt, you can speak very softly, because you've got the biggest stick (army) in town.

References

1   John 16:33

2   Philippians 4:9

3   Romans 5:3-4

4   Hebrews 10:23

5   Matthew 7:14

6   I John 4:18

7   Psalms 50:14

8   Psalms 112:7

9   James 4:9-10

10 II Timothy 1:7

11 Psalms 37:8

12 Psalms 118:5-6

13 Matthew 6:33

14 Luke 12:25

15 Matthew 6:34

16 Luke 9:62 (NIV)

17 II Corinthians 11:14-15

18 A person who "goes for" this and "goes for" that.

19 Jeremiah 29:13

20 Philippians 4:6

21 Ephesians 6:18

22 I Thessalonians 5:18

23 Hebrews 4:16

24 Philippians 4:13

25 Philippians 4:8

26 James 4:7

27 Romans 8:39

28   II Kings 6:16

29   Psalms 62:1,6-7

Chapter 8

Come Fly
With Me!

The morning was overcast, dull, and gray. It was the kind of morning that affected my mood, made me feel down. From all appearances, there was a good chance of rain to further complicate the day for everyone. I was glad to be getting out early, leaving this mess for someone else to solve.

The weather briefing report indicated the current conditions—low overcast. It also reported the cloud layer was only a few hundred feet thick and by mid morning would "burn" off from the sun's warmth. The forecast projected sunny skies and pleasantly warm.

However, the reports left me unprepared for the special treat that was in store for me on this particular day. Our crew went methodically through the routine of flight preparation and was "building our nests" in the close comfort of the cockpit.

At departure time we pushed back, started the engines, and taxied out to the active runway. Shortly, we were given our clearance for takeoff and we began our roll toward flight. We lifted off and quickly tucked the gear away. The wheels barely made it into the wheel wells before we hit the thick gray of the overcast. It was all instruments now—those little gauges that made certain we kept the "sunny side up."

As we neared the top of the overcast, the gray began to dispel. We burst through the tops and the scene which met our eyes was spectacular. The sun was just peeking over the overcast. Its rays skimmed across the tops in an array of colors that defied description. Because of the jet's climb rate, the clouds seemed to fall away vertically. This hurried the sunrise, causing everything to move in accelerated motion. We barely had time to assimilate one scene before our senses were flooded with another and another and another wonderful display.

We were spellbound. Thirty minutes passed before anyone spoke. We knew we had just witnessed something special and were reluctant to interrupt our musings. It was going to be a great day after all.

Little did we know this was only the beginning. It was a long day. The last leg took us from Dallas to Las Vegas. High above the Rockies in our lofty perch, we surveyed our kingdom. Visibility seemed endless. There was no haze today. The horizon in front of us was so crisp it seemed only miles away. The sun was nearing the horizon.

For some reason, I remembered an article I had read years before. It described the phenomena of the "green flash." A sunset combined with clear atmospheric conditions, in the last micro-second the sun disappears over the horizon, can produce a magnificent "emerald green flash." This phenomena is so rare only a few humans have ever witnessed it, and primarily only those who live in the clear, unpolluted elevations of the Himalayan mountains. After describing this to the crew, we decided we were higher than any mountain, the day was crystal clear, so we might as well watch. But the article had warned, "Don't blink, for if you do, you may well

100   Come Fly
                                              With Me!

miss one of natures amazing wonders." The sun sank lower and lower, until only a sliver remained. We dared not blink. Our eyes burned. If we could help it, we were not going to miss it.

Suddenly, clearly, it happened! The brilliance of the green was stunning. We had once again seen God's hand at work. It had been a long day, but we felt refreshed and very special. It was so good to be alive.

But how had I arrived at this day?

The words which follow are my personal testimony. They were born during a time of emotional pain. The exact circumstance does not matter. Of greater importance is my discovery.

No matter what the situation—rejection and abandonment, death of a loved one, terminal illness, abuse, or whatever else life unexpectedly throws at us **He can be trusted with our hopes, our future, and our eternal well-being.**

Most of the time there is no instant solution. However, if we allow Him to work out His purpose in our lives, it will bring peace to troubled minds and rest to exhausted bodies. As I allowed the Holy Spirit to work in my life, He gently helped me progress. Without Him I do not know where I would be. With each new day, I must actuate His mercy and grace for today. My tomorrows must remain in His hands.

When I read, *No matter what happens, ALWAYS be thankful, for this is God's will for you who belong to Christ Jesus,* [1] I felt the old missionary must have taken temporary leave of his senses. But had he?

Immersed in the conflicts of a fiery trial which seemed to threaten my very existence, this statement was absolutely formidable. James pressed the point even further when he implied the only emotion we should allow during times of difficulty is happiness. *Is your life full of difficulties and temptations? Then be happy!* [2]

Quite frankly, when my fingernails are bloody from just barely hanging on emotionally, the last thing I can think of is happiness. I'd be happy with simple survival, but happiness? Get real!

More accurately, *He has...given me a cup of deepest sorrows to drink—he has rolled me in ashes and dirt. O Lord, all peace and all prosperity have long since gone, for you have taken them away. I have forgotten what enjoyment is. All hope is gone; my strength has turned to water, for the Lord has left me.* [3] I know exactly how David felt when he said *I am upset and disturbed. My mind is filled with apprehension and with gloom—I am worn out with pain; every night my pillow is wet with tears. My eyes are growing old and dim with grief*[4]

In 1982, circumstance had drastically altered the course of my life. A career had gone up in smoke. I was able to make the transition to the international business environment. Things went well for a short time, then suddenly, events brought my castle crashing down. I knew the time had come to examine my priorities and set fresh goals. I had put God on the back burner for too long.

For five months, I lived in a country whose language I could not speak. The isolation provided an atmosphere for self-examination. Upon return to the States, I put in motion the goals I had set. However, the more I tried, the worse things got until finally, crisis! At first, self-justification and excuses; then the self-condemnation of "If only" set in.

I retreated to the only shelter I could find, prayer and reading His Word. Momentarily, the scriptures opened. It seemed that one promise was just for me. *For I know the plans I have for you, says the Lord. They are plans for good and not for evil, to give you a future and a hope...* [5]

Then with a finality I had never experienced, the Word turned to dust. Prayer bounced back in my face, emphasizing my isolation and vulnerability. Images of happiness enjoyed by others taunted me wherever I went. Someone was playing a horrible joke on me, mocking my hurt. The more I turned to the Word, prayer, and listening to Christian television, the more isolated I felt. Words of help and encouragement from loved ones only exaggerated the problem.

I reminded God of the commitments I had made, but it seemed apparent He wasn't interested. My reminders became more intense. "How could You, God? How could You put this added trip on me?" Because of this perceived rejection, I became angry, really angry! I would cry out in the silence of my apartment the frustration and anger I felt with God. But when that failed to impress Him, my anger turned to desperation. I clung to the one scripture I felt He had given me.

One day, something else managed to penetrate the fog that surrounded me. That promise went on to say, *in those days when you pray, I will listen.* "OK, then where in the world have you been, God? Turn the hearing aid up; I'm in trouble. PLEASE!" Finally the last phrase sank in. *You will find me when you seek me, if you look for me in earnest* At first I barely recognized the implication. Slowly but surely, the

Holy Spirit gently kept imprinting those words into my subconscious.

Desperation does not necessarily mean you are in earnest. My commitments had been honest but also superficial. I wanted to hedge my bets with God. "O.K. God, I'm yours, but I also want..." Another thought began to materialize. Years before I remembered hearing how *Abraham believed God, and that is why God cancelled his sins and declared him 'not guilty'.* [6] Either I believed God's promise or I didn't. How could I "believe God" when I didn't even know if He was listening, let alone speaking to me? The mental arguments went on and on. Slowly it became apparent I must either "put up or shut up" and put my money where my mouth was. I began to be aware I was facing my "High Noon."

My phone bill soared (Ma Bell loved me) because of my desperate (all hours of the night and day) calls to Mom and Dad. How I thank God for parents who knew how to reach Heaven! Dad tried his best to encourage and support. Then late one night, possibly out of sheer desperation, he spoke words that were truly from Heaven. He said, "Son, just start PRAISING Him!"

"You're joking, right? Give me a break! Praise? I can't even pray. God hasn't even been considerate enough to let me know He even cares, let alone exists. How in the name of anything sensible do you expect me to PRAISE Him?"

But like all seeds planted in His will, the Holy Spirit has this gentle but persistent way of getting it through from concept to action. For several days, I battled this "High Noon."

Driving down a crowded freeway during rush hour is not the ideal place to stage a showdown with God, but that is exactly

---

where it took place. He must have known I was finally totally honest and *in EARNEST*, and put His guardian angels around me that day.

In bumper-to-bumper traffic, tears of emotional depression streamed down my face as I talked to God in the privacy of my car. The emotional pain was so great death would have been a relief. I remembered Job's commitment. In desperation I simply stated, "O.K. God, You win. I am going to trust You."

I am sure my Heavenly Father must have had a good chuckle at the next three words. In spite of what I felt and in defiance of the frustration, I said the words, "I praise You!" It was anything but praise. But God respects an honest heart. The words were simply a step of faith, but I will never forget the impact it had upon me.

As I spoke those words, tears burst with such intensity I literally could not see. For the first time in months, the skies opened. His love surrounded me with such intensity I felt I could not bear it. I was indeed on Holy Ground. From deep within, I was able to really and honestly praise Him; not for the circumstance, but in spite of it, for who and what He is.

What a change took place! Where the Word had been like dust, suddenly it seemed on every page there was a verse just for me. Where praying had been a one-sided, seemingly futile effort on my part, now I felt His presence as never before.

Where anger had stood, it was gone. *He is for me! How can I be afraid? What can mere man do to me?* [7] When I make a mistake, He is faithful to help me. Where I once stood defenseless, I now have the ability to resist. If we *resist the devil—he WILL flee from us...* [8] Where anxiety once filled my being, I now have the admonition to not ...*worry about anything; instead, pray about everything; tell God your needs and don't forget to thank Him for the answers. If you do this you will experience God's peace, which is far more wonderful than the human mind can understand. His peace will keep your thoughts and your hearts quiet and at rest as you trust in Christ Jesus.* [9] Finally, I can let Him have all my worries, because I know that ...*He is always thinking about [me] and watching everything that concerns [me].* [10]

But I had been on the defensive. In any battle, as "Dandy Don" Meredith on Monday night football used to say, "Old Mo' changes sides." Momentum or initiative is usually not on the same side as the defense. There comes a point when the Holy Spirit can trust us to actively participate in our own defense.

By faith, we begin to see the answer we are searching for. Faith is ...*the confident assurance that something we want is going to happen. It is the certainty that what we hope for is waiting for us, even though we cannot see it up ahead.* [11] But we must activate faith, because *faith that doesn't show itself by good works is no faith at all—it is dead and useless.* [12]

I am convinced the Holy Spirit revealed the concept of "WAR PRAISE."

WAR PRAISE is aggressive praise that is given when we just can't praise, when everything is wrong, when there is no apparent reason to praise Him, when the night is blackest. It is praise given to Him simply because I believe His Word, even when all the evidence points to the contrary. It is not praise for a circumstance or trial. It is praise which I give to the Father for Who He is, praise that I give in spite of the circumstance, praise that is due Him because of what

He did for me at Calvary, and for what He is doing in my life. Remembering the words, "Just PRAISE Him," which my Dad spoke late that night, I realized the intricate, yet wonderfully simple puzzle, the Holy Spirit was putting together to bring me to this point. For the first time, I am just beginning to understand how much He really loves me and why I can trust Him completely with my life.

For some, the storm is short, but for others, long and intense. At some point, hope ceases to exist. The light at the end of the tunnel goes out. The time for games is over—it's now life or death. You have reached your "High Noon." The time has come to decide which side you are on. The possibility of fence-sitting no longer exists. Your enemy can see and smell his victory. He thinks he has won; you are on the defensive, just hanging on by your fingernails. He presses in for the kill.

In the city one day, *a mob was quickly formed.. the judges ordered them stripped and beaten with wooden whips. Again and again the rods slashed down across their bared backs; and afterwards they were thrown into prison. The jailer was threatened with death if they escaped, so he took no chances, but put them into the inner dungeon and clamped their feet into the stocks.* [13] It's not a pretty picture. There is every reason to question "WHY?" and good enough reason to quit. Or is there?

Be sure of this, that He will listen to us whenever we ask Him for anything in line with His will. And if we really know He is listening when we talk to Him and make our requests, then we can be sure that He will answer us. [14]

Daniel was in the middle of a fast, waiting for an answer that did not appear to be on its way. Suddenly...*there before me stood a person robed in linen garments.. from his face came blinding flashes like lightning, and his eyes were pools of fire...I grew pale and weak with fright...* When Daniel regained control of his senses, the messenger gave him the message, *Don't be frightened, Daniel, for your request has been heard in heaven and was answered the very first day you began to fast before the Lord and pray.. that very day I was sent here to meet you. But for twenty one days the mighty Evil Spirit who overrules the kingdom of Persia blocked my way. Then Michael, one of the top officers of the heavenly army, came to help me, so that I was able to break through these spirit rulers.* [15] *You see, we are not fighting against people made of flesh and blood, but against persons without bodies, the evil rulers of the unseen world, those mighty satanic beings and great evil princes of darkness who rule this world.* [16]

When we are in the middle of our battle, up to our necks in the slippery marsh that threatens to engulf and overwhelm us, we lose sight of our primary objective—to bring glory and honor to our Creator. Others are not **persuaded** to Christ through reason or argument, but are **drawn** to Him when they see genuine love and grace as a reality. It is when we reflect His grace and His love that others are attracted to Him.

When I am down and barely hanging in there, how can I possibly do anything but just survive? His answer resounds through the empty and lonely hours because *I am with you; that is all you need. My power shows up best in weak people.* [17] When we are self-sufficient, we get in the way. When we acknowledge our lack of skill, our weakness, and our dependency on Him, it provides Him the opportunity to demonstrate His care for His very own.

Meanwhile, back at the city—in prison, beaten, bruised, misused, falsely accused and with a bleak future outlook,

Come Fly
With Me!

Paul and Silas remained. In those painful and lonely hours after the beating, I am sure the tendency to question was there. But there was no cause for worry. The reinforcements had not yet been called, the Battle Cry had not yet been sounded. Instead, there in the darkness, they began to consider why they were there, who they were, and to Whom they belonged. As those thoughts began to fill their minds, and the magnitude of His love filled their very beings, slowly but surely WAR PRAISE began.

It was *around midnight, as Paul and Silas were PRAYING and SINGING HYMNS to the Lord. Suddenly there was a great earthquake; the prison was shaken to its foundations, all* the *doors flew open—and the chains of every prisoner fell off!* [18]

When you begin your WAR PRAISE, look out! Be ready! Things are about to happen. The commanders of all the evil forces are hastily sounding retreat. Satan is scrambling out of his bunker and running for cover. He knows the gauntlet has just been thrown. Enough is enough! Heaven's Supreme Commander has called in the heavy artillery. He's coming through. His Child needs Him! He is calling to me, "Hang in there, kid, I'm on my way! Just hang on!"

The rulers of darkness may delay, but they cannot stop your answers from coming. As we begin to PRAISE our Heavenly Father, there is no force on earth that can prevent Him from inhabiting the praise of His child. *I am convinced that nothing can separate us from His love. Death can't, and life can't. The angels won't, and all the powers of hell itself cannot keep God's love away. Our fears for today, our worries about tomorrow, or where we are—high in the sky, or in the deepest ocean—nothing, nothing, NOTHING will ever be able to separate us from the love of God.* [19]

In the center of the storm, all the forces of heaven under the command of the King of Glory, came to my assistance. My WAR PRAISE had become the battle cry for the forces of Heaven. My PRAISE had opened the way for Heaven's forces to stream through the breach to my side. *Open up, O ancient gates, and let the King of Glory in. Who is this King of Glory? The Lord, strong and mighty, invincible in battle. Yes, open wide the gates and let the King of Glory in. Who is this King of Glory? THE COMMANDER OF ALL OF HEAVEN'S ARMIES!* [20]

That's right! I don't have just an angel as in Daniel's case. I have the COMMANDER Himself rushing to my assistance to hold me tenderly in his loving arms, stroking away my hurts, picking me up, and putting my feet back on the ground, providing me with a *hope and a future.*

"Oh thank you, Lord Jesus, for this wonderful hope, the light at the end of my tunnel, Your hand which holds me up even as I fall and stumble along a path I have not traveled before, Your presence in the dark and frightening hours of the night. Thank you for providing the silver lining to the clouds which seem to hover so oppressively over me. Thank you for allowing me to be Your child, for Your care and love. Thank you for relieving my anxiety because You will *take care of my tomorrow.* [21] Thank you for taking my worries and cares because *You are always thinking about me and watching everything that concerns me.* [22] Thank you for that place of refuge that is provided when I am willing to completely trust You. Thank you for giving me the ability to PRAISE YOU, even when it seems impossible. Thank you for allowing Your grace to break through all the barriers the evil forces put in place, defeating them and providing victory. Thank You for the peace which keeps my *thoughts and [my] heart quiet and at rest,* [23] providing rest from the deep anxiety which accompanies the unknown. But most of all, thank you for allowing me to see that you are accomplishing some higher purpose in my life. Even though I do not know where it will lead, I can trust you completely. Thank you for your ability to see that there is something worth salvaging in my life. Oh, King of Glory and MY Father, thank you! Thank you! THANK YOU!"

Thank you for allowing me to FLY AGAIN!

References

1   I Thessalonians 5:18

2   James 1:2

3   Jeremiah 3:15-18

4   Psalms 6

5   Lamentations 29:11

6   Romans 4:3

7   Psalms 118:6

8   James 4:7

9   Philippians 4:6-7

10   I Peter 5:7

11   Hebrews 11:1

12   James 2:17

13   Acts 16:22-24

14   I John 5:14-15

15   Daniel 10

16   Ephesians 6:12

17   II Corinthians 12:9

18   Acts 16:25-26

19   Romans 8:38-39

20   Psalms 24:7-10

21   Matthew 6:34

22   I Peter 5:7

23   Philippians 4:7

Chapter 9

Luther's Dilemma

What does a young law student, born in 1483, who changed his major from law to theology, have to do with me? Martin Luther received his ordination in 1507. Everything was going well. Goals were being realized. Then suddenly, crisis!

His world was shaken as he observed the lack of moral integrity in the leaders of the church. As a result of and through his study of scripture, he developed strong doubts about to his salvation. He began to wonder if he was not quite good enough to measure up to what God expected. To him, his eternal destiny was now in question. His world began to crumble, and his life's work began to appear meaningless.

What could change this picture of dejection into the German leader of the Protestant Reformation? What could change this man with personal anxiety into the assured leader who posted his historic 95 Theses to the door of the castle church, endangering his own life? What could reverse his lack of confidence so much that he translated the New Testament into German and began a translation of the entire Bible? How could personal crisis change into powerful writings and preaching, read and heard throughout his world?

Unlike every other page of this book, this chapter may be the most important one you will ever read. Of all the decisions required in life, nothing compares in importance with the one presented here. Without resolution, all other themes in this book are meaningless.

People like to have answers in advance. If we don't have everything figured out, we often remain skeptical. More than anyone, Jesus understood this human necessity to rationalize before we commit. *It is easier for a camel to go through the eye of a needle than for a rich man to enter the Kingdom of God.* [1] He further explained that *anyone who will not receive the kingdom of God like a little child will never enter it.* [2]

Does that mean that we should blindly follow some "religion" with mindless, simplistic trust? Absolutely not! Recently we have seen the tragic results of this kind of "trust." Self-proclaimed "messiahs" can never point to prophesies fulfilled, the lame walking, the blind seeing, and emotions healed. On the contrary, the honest, seeking mind that examines the evidence, will find it overwhelmingly in favor of His message and life.

"It is evidence of His [Christ's] importance…that no other life ever lived on this planet has evoked so huge a volume of literature among so many peoples and languages, and that, far from ebbing, **the flood continues to mount.**" [3]

Napoleon, the great general and leader of men, stated, "I know men; and I tell you that Jesus Christ is not a man. Superficial minds see a resemblance between Christ and the founders of empires, and the gods of other religions. That resemblance does not exist. There is between Christianity and whatever other religions, the distance of infinity…Everything in Christ astonishes me. His spirit overawes me, and His will confounds me. Between him and whoever else in the world, there is no possible term of comparison. He is truly a being by himself. His ideas and sentiments, the truth which He announces, his manner of convincing, are not explained either by human organization or by the nature of things...**His religion is a revelation from an intelligence which certainly is not that of man...One can absolutely find nowhere, but in him alone, the imitation or the example of his life...I search in vain in history to find a similar to Jesus Christ, or anything which can approach the gospel.** Neither history, nor humanity, nor the ages, nor nature, offer me anything with which I am able to compare it or to explain it. Here everything is extraordinary."[4]

History recorded Voltaire's proclamations that Christianity would no longer exist within one hundred years. This French infidel died in 1778. Jesus on the other hand said, *My word...will achieve the purpose for which I sent it.* [5] Voltaire has passed into history. Yet mounting evidence continues to point to the Messiah, the Savior of mankind. (See note [6])

However, mankind is still searching to fill in the blanks. Where have we come from and where are we going? We still want to know.

How Can I Know The Way?

It was just that question to which Jesus responded when He stated, *I am the way the truth and the life. No one comes to the Father except through me.* [7] He knew there would be some who would not accept His way and how costly this rejection would be. *How does a man benefit if he gains the whole world and loses his soul in the process?* [8]

Why Is Salvation (Spiritual Rebirth) Necessary?

Jesus said it was necessary.

If a person is morally good, endeavors to do what is right, believes in God, attends church, gives to the poor, and does all the other things that men usually believe to be the criteria for attaining acceptance by God, is that good enough?

A very important man named Nicodemus, a member of the ruling council of the synagogue, came to Jesus secretly one night. He wanted to avoid being seen by his peers. He asked the same question. *Jesus replied, 'With all the earnestness I possess I tell you this: Unless you are born again, you can never get into the Kingdom of God.'* [9] He went on to explain that just as a person must be born physically, so must he experience spiritual birth.

What Was It That Martin Luther Discovered?

He knew that *God so loved the world that He gave His one and only Son, that whoever believes in Him shall not perish but have eternal life.* [10] He was familiar with the words of Isaiah when he described what the sacrifice at Calvary would mean to each person. *He was pierced for our transgressions, he was crushed for our iniquities; the punishment that brought us peace was upon him, and by his wounds we are healed.* [11]

But as he read further, he found that *all our righteous acts are like filthy rags...and like the wind our sins sweep us away.* [12] In fact, in God's eyes *there is no one righteous, not even one...* [13] And if that were not enough, he read *all have sinned and fall short of the glory of God* [14] He found that *the wages of sin is death, but the gift of God is eternal life.* [15] Worse yet, *man is destined to die once, and after that to face judgment.* [16]

Not a pretty picture. Not only is our own righteousness like so many filthy rags, but we have all sinned. The result of sin is death (meaning eternal separation from God), and we will face judgment for those sins. Humanly, this is an impossible picture, a "no win" situation.

Is There Anything That I Can Do About It?

It was this dilemma that drove Martin Luther to search for an answer. How could he obtain forgiveness for himself and be good enough for God to accept him?

Luther understood that *God demonstrate(d) his own love for us in this: While we were still sinners, Christ died for us.* [17] Because of His sacrifice, *whoever believes in Him (the Messiah) is not condemned, but whoever does not believe stands condemned already because he has not believed in the name of God's one and only Son.* [18]

God is only concerned about one thing. What decision have you made relative to your relationship with His Son, Jesus Christ? It is not our good works or our efforts that impress Him. *It is by grace you (are) saved, through faith...it is the gift of God—not by works, so that no one can boast.* [19]

We can do something about it. In spite of our "no win" position, with a simple act of faith we can realize God's forgiveness and His promise of eternal life.

But How Do I Activate This Faith?

One day, Jesus told his disciples that His plan for salvation was so simple that not even a child could make a mistake. He explained that all it takes is to *confess with your mouth, 'Jesus is Lord,' and believe in your heart that God raised him from the dead, you will be saved. For it is with your heart that you believe and are justified, and it is with your mouth that you confess and are saved. Everyone who calls on the name of the Lord will be saved.* [20]

That's it, just that simple to find peace and the assurance of eternal life. But Martin Luther knew all this. Yet somehow there was still a vital missing link.

What Was This Missing Link?

One day as he read, he encountered the capsule summary of Paul's message to the Romans. It changed his life forever. For the first time, he read and understood the phrase, *righteousness from God*. Realizing the total concept of spiritual birth, he exclaimed, "This passage of Paul became to me a gateway to heaven."

It was no longer necessary for him to determine if he was good enough to be accepted. *This **righteousness from God** comes through faith in Jesus Christ to all who believe.* [21] It was not his righteousness, but the fact that once he *believed in [his] heart* and *confess[ed] with [his] mouth*, righteousness was no longer his responsibility. He no longer had to wonder if he was good enough to be accepted by God.

Instead, God allows the sacrifice made at Calvary to enable Him (Jesus) to *become...our righteousness, holiness and redemption.* [22] As one insightful person observed, "God no longer looks at our righteousness and sees filthy rags, but puts on glasses which have a 'Jesus' filter. Through this filter, He sees not our filthy rags, but the righteousness of His Son who is now our righteousness!"

So What's In It For Us—You And I?

Therefore, since we have been justified through faith, we have PEACE with God through our Lord Jesus Christ. [23] *For God so loved the world that He gave his one and only Son, that whoever believes in Him shall not perish but have eternal life.* [24]

That's what we get—the PEACE of knowing our eternal destiny and ETERNAL LIFE!

Would You Like To Experience This PEACE?

Jesus said, *I stand at the door [of your heart] and knock. If anyone hears my voice and opens the door, I will come in and [share] with [them], and [they] with me.* [25]

You must invite Him into your life. He is too polite to ever intrude. If you would like to invite Him to be your Savior, you may use this simple prayer.

"Dear God, I believe that Jesus is Lord; I accept Jesus sacrifice on the cross which He made for me. I believe that He rose again and is now with You. I ask that You forgive me of my sins, and accept me as Your child. I will, with Your help, endeavor to live as You want me to. I accept this by faith because I trust Your Word. I ask this in Jesus' name. Amen."

What Happens Now?

One day Jesus was teaching, and concluded by saying, *there is joy in the presence of the angels of God when one sinner repents.* [26] The very next thing is that an angel records your name in the *Lamb's Book of Life.*

In the book of Revelation is the description of a wonderful city built by God. The walls are made of jasper, the foundations have every form of precious stone, and the streets are made of pure gold like transparent glass. It is also very specific as to who can enter that city. *Nothing impure will ever enter it, nor will any one who does what is shameful or deceitful, but only those whose names are written in the Lamb's Book of Life.* [27]

Pretty fantastic! Quite a difference from that "no win" position.

Someday, I hope to meet you in that city. So long for now and *HAPPY FLYING!*

References

1   Luke 18:25 NIV

2   Luke 18:17 NIV

3   Kenneth Scott Latourette, former Yale historian, A History of Christianity. New York: Harper & Row, 1953, pg 44. Used by permission.

4   Cited by Vernon C. Grounds, The Reason for Our Hope. Chicago: Moody Press, 1945, pg 37. Used by permission.

5   Isaiah 55:11 NIV

6   Peter's statement, "Always be prepared to give an answer..." (I Peter 3:15), has prompted many to study books which document evidence of Biblical authenticity. Using this documentation to "prove" arguments, is in this author's opinion, a fruitless exercise. Only the Holy Spirit can convince of the need for a Savior.

    Rather, when this evidence is used to build your own faith, confidence will reflect in your stated reasons when questioned about your faith. Several books provide excellent insights, such as The Battle for the Bible, Harold Lindsell, Zondervan Publishing House and Encyclopedia of Bible Difficulties, Gleason L. Archer, Zondervan Publishing House. However, one that has been a special blessing to the author, is Evidence That Demands a Verdict, Josh McDowell, Campus Crusade for Christ, Inc.

7   John 14:6 NIV

8   Mark 8:36

9   John 3:3

10 John 3:16 NIV

11 Isaiah 53:5 NIV

12 Isaiah 64:6 NIV

13 Romans 3:10 NIV

14 Romans 3:23 NIV

15 Romans 6:23 NIV

16 Hebrews 9:27 NIV

17 Romans 5:8 NIV

18 John 3:18 NIV

19 Ephesians 2:8-9 NIV

20 Romans 10:9-10, 13 NIV

21 Romans 3:22 NIV

22 I Corinthians 1:30 NIV

23 Romans 5:1 NIV

24 John 3:16 NIV

25 Revelation 3:20 NIV

26 Luke 15:10

27 Revelation 21:27 NIV

Some Really Important Stuff

You arrived at the crossroad. You made your decision. You decided to enter the *small* gate and travel *the road [that] is narrow* [1] which leads to Life. In other words, you just started your journey as a Christian.

This decision was not a one-time action. In reality, you have started an adventure which will last the rest of your life. Now you must *be a good workman, one who does not need to be ashamed when God examines your work.* [2] Your new relationship with God must be developed and nourished. God knows you, but now you must get to know Him intimately. To help you accomplish this, I have provided a few suggestions.

Talk to God DAILY.

Too often we use prayer as a time to give God our "want" list. We give Him time only when we want or need something. God, on the other hand, wants our companionship and worship. He desires our time with Him in prayer, time in which He can also speak to us.

Jesus provided a good example to follow when we approach God in prayer. [3] First, we should give Him praise and honor for who He is, and thank Him for all He has done for us. Our praise and thanksgiving let Him know we are mindful of His presence in our lives. After our offering of worship, allow Him the time during our quiet time to speak to us through His Word. Now we can ask Him for our needs.

Learn to use "dead time". [4] Use this time to worship **without** asking Him for anything. Just think about Him, the things He has done for you, and offer your praise to Him. You will be amazed at the transformation in your prayer life.

Scriptures to get you started:

- Revelation 3:20; II Corinthians 5:17; John 10:10; John 1:11, 12; Colossians 1:13, 14; Colossians 1:26, 27

Let God Talk to You.

Your Bible is God's Reference Manual. It is His primary method of communication, His personal phone line direct to your heart. His *Word...will achieve the purpose for which [He] sent it.* [5] When His Word touches our hearts, it is never without purpose.

Since most of us are not Biblical scholars previously exposed to the seventeenth century English used in the King James Bible, it is sometimes difficult to grasp the wonderful meanings of a particular verse. For this reason, I have and use three Bible translations.

- The first is the King James Version (KJV). Reason: Many Bible study aids, such as Strong's Concordance and others, are cross referenced to words used in this version. Therefore, when searching for a particular reference or the original meaning of a Greek or Hebrew word, this version is a must.

- The second is the New International Version (NIV). I am partial to this one because it uses modern-day English, yet closely retains the accuracy of the original text. I chose the NIV Student Bible because of notes inserted at key locations which provide helpful insight to authors, books, places, and things.

- Finally, The Living Bible (TLB). I used it almost exclusively throughout this book. Reason: it often most eloquently expresses in easy to understand terms, meanings of a particular verse or passage. An excellent example of this clarity of expression is, *You have collected all my tears and preserved them in your bottle!* [6] I understand that kind analogy, showing the depth of God's care for my hurts.

For those of you with a computer, available Bible study software can be used to maximize your study time. Several good products are on the market in a variety of formats and price. I personally use the PC Study Bible™ by Biblesoft.[7] This should not be considered an endorsement, as you may find another product which serves your requirements better. However, the reasons I chose this particular software are:

- It runs under either DOS™ or Windows™; Windows makes it easier, of course.

- It contains a Concordance with a "word search" capability. This allows me to find all verses which contain that word or words quickly and efficiently. It will search the complete Bible in just a few seconds.

- It has all the above versions of the Bible and more. Once I have located a particular verse (probably in the King James version), by pressing just one key, I can view the New International translation. If I press the key again, I see The Living Bible rendition or I can see all three of them, side by side.

- If I want to start a set of notes, it has its own built-in Notepad (like a simple word processor). With one keystroke I can copy a whole verse into it or type in my own notes.

- It contains Nave's Topical Bible, Nelson's Bible Dictionary, Vine's Expository Dictionary, Strong's Greek/Hebrew Dictionary, and Englishman's Concordance. All are vital and excellent tools to help expand my study horizons.

- However, the most important reason I use computer software is very simple—EFFICIENCY. I can cover so much more material effectively, maximizing precious study time.

Why are the two communication steps listed above so important? Because this is how you grow spiritually.

More scriptures to keep you going:

- I Peter 5:7, 8; John 15:7; John 14:21; Matthew 4:19; John 15:8; Acts 1:8; Galatians 5:16, 17

Finally,

Find A GOOD Church Home.

The Apostle Paul [8] urges us not to neglect the *assembling of ourselves together*. We all need a support group. But you must be sure the church you choose honors Christ and that His Word is honored.

How do we know it's a good church? The Psalmist stated, *I have hidden your Word in my heart that I might not sin against you.* [9] If we have not read His Word, how can we hide it in our hearts for future use? This is the reason it is so important for us to read His Word daily. If we do this faithfully, the Holy Spirit can then recall His Words to our hearts and minds at the appropriate times to help us answer life's questions. Now, *His Spirit speaks to us deep in our hearts* [10] and we know when His Word is being taught with truth and clarity, without compromise. Part of our growth is learning to be sensitive to His Word.

Your spiritual welfare is your responsibility, not the preacher's or the priest's. Even the people at Beroea *searched the scriptures day by day to check up on Paul and Silas' statements to see if they were really so.* [11]

Remember, His Word comforts, encourages, and guides. But the *Word of God is living and active.* It is *sharper than any double-edged sword.. judg[ing] the thoughts and attitudes of the heart.* [12] This means it will also challenge us in our daily lives. If the Holy Spirit finds some corner of our hearts or lives that need work, He will use God's Word to prick our hearts with conviction. As we respond, growth becomes reality. Slowly but surely, the "gold" of our lives is refined to insure we become more like Him, reflecting with true clarity His meaningful intervention.

My Prayer.

Search me, O God, and know my heart; test my thoughts. Point out anything you find in me that makes you sad, and lead me along the path of everlasting life. [13]

Amen!

References

1   Mathew 7:14

2   II Timothy 2:15

3   Matthew 6:9

4   I define "dead time" as time when I am limited or confined, unable to do anything other than just sit or wait. However, I can still think; my mind can be active. Commuting in any mode of transportation or waiting for appointments, are just two examples of "dead time."

5   Isaiah 55:11 NIV

6   Psalms 56:8

7   Copyright by Biblesoft, Seattle, Washington, (800) 995-9058

8   Hebrews 10:25

9   Psalms 119:11 NIV

10   Romans 8:16

11   Acts 17:11

12   Hebrews 4:12 NIV

13   Psalms 139:23, 24